You, Your Marriage, Your Kids

Anthony Ferraioli, M.D.

CONTENTS

Introduction pg.13

　A Brand New Collection of Essays

Chapter 1 pg.17

　How to Live a Peaceful Life (Y)

Chapter 2 pg.21

　Dealing with Chronic Fear and with Anticipatory Anxiety (Y)

Chapter 3 pg.27

　You Can't Get 'Past' What You Haven't Been 'Through' (Y)

Chapter 4 pg.33

　Being Where You're Supposed To Be (Y)

Chapter 5 pg.40

　Forgiveness in Your Marriage (M)

Chapter 6 pg.45

　An LVAC Primer (K)

Chapter 7 pg.52

　Chronic Anger (Y)

Chapter 8 pg.58

  Creating Happy Memories (K)

Chapter 9 pg.63

  Do You Treat Your Spouse as You Would Want Your Child to be Treated by Theirs? (M)

Chapter 10 pg.69

  Do You DO Free Time? (Y)

Chapter 11 pg.74

  A Time to Talk (K)

Chapter 12 pg.78

  Idealization and Disappointment in Dating and Marriage (M)

Chapter 13 pg.85

  YOU Are First (Y)

Chapter 14 pg.92

  Emotional Credibility (Y)

Chapter 15 pg.96

  Is Your Spouse a Stranger or "Family" (M)

Chapter 16 pg.102

  Adult Neutrality (Y)

Chapter 17 pg.107

How to Reverse Time (K)

Chapter 18 pg.113

Coming in for a Landing: Time and Money in Your Marriage (M)

Chapter 19 pg.117

Are the Holidays 'Happy' for You? (Y)

Chapter 20 pg.122

Becoming an 'Active Listener' (Y)

Chapter 21 pg.126

Man-Boys and Angry Wives (M)

Chapter 22 pg.132

Contentment vs. Ambition: Why Not Both? (Y)

Chapter 23 pg.136

Building Emotional Credibility With Your Teen (K)

Chapter 24 pg.141

Marital Expectations (M)

Chapter 25 pg.146

Does Your Work Help Make You a Better Person? (Y)

Chapter 26 pg.150

LVAC for Asperger's (K)

Chapter 27 pg.157

　Marriage is an Emotional Laboratory (M)

Chapter 28 pg.161

　Don't Go to a Hot Rod Shop for an Oil Change (Y)

Chapter 29 pg.169

　LVAC Stance (K)

Chapter 30 pg.172

　Saying 'I'm Sorry' (M)

Chapter 31 pg.178

　Emotional Fat on the Bone (Y)

Chapter 32 pg.184

　The Lid and the Boiling Pot (K)

Chapter 33 pg.189

　Sex and Marriage (M)

Chapter 34 pg.194

　Engagement in Your Life (Y)

Chapter 35 pg.201

　The Danger of Making Generalizations (K)

Chapter 36 pg.206

　The Marriage Problem (M)

Chapter 37 pg.211

　　Healthy Self-Esteem (Y)

Chapter 38 pg.216

　　The Emotional Weather System Around You (M)

Chapter 39 pg.221

　　Trust by the Pound (Y)

Chapter 40 pg.225

　　How Being Stuck Can Cause Other Problems (Y)

Chapter 41 pg.229

　　The Extraordinary Spirit of Children (K)

Chapter 42 pg.236

　　Unconditional Love vs. Unconditional Positive Regard (M)

Chapter 43 pg.241

　　How to Help Somebody Calm Down (Y)

Chapter 44 pg.245

　　What Legacy Will You Leave? (K)

Chapter 45 pg.250

　　Why We Marry Who We Do (M)

Chapter 46 pg.256

Who is in the Words that You Speak? (Y)

Chapter 47 pg.260

Us Compared to Our Parents (K)

Chapter 48 pg.265

Losing Your Happy (Y)

Chapter 49 pg.269

Why it's Important to LVAC with your Child (K)

Chapter 50 pg.274

Keeping your Core..While Making an Impact (Y)

Chapter 51 pg.277

What is the Story You Tell Yourself about Your Kids? (K)

Chapter 52 pg.283

Listening Builds Hope (Y)

Chapter 53 pg.288

Will Your Kids Visit You in the Nursing Home? (K)

Chapter 54 pg.294

The Long Goodbye: How the Acknowledgement of Death can Help Us Really Live (Y)

Chapter 55 pg.299

Not Acting Like a Victim (Y)

Chapter 56 pg.303

  Raising Victims (K)

Chapter 57 pg.308

  Settling Down (M)

Chapter 58 pg.313

  Seeking to Truly Understand (Y)

Chapter 59 pg.317

  The Side-Effects of Chronic Multitasking (Y)

Chapter 60 pg.320

  The One Minute Trick (Y)

Chapter 61 pg.323

  Learning to Stop (Y)

Chapter 62 pg.328

  REALADULTS (Y)

Chapter 63 pg.335

  Living Deliberately (Y)

Chapter 64 pg.341

  How to Identify Pain (Y)

Chapter 65 pg.346

  The Problem with Our Addictions (Y)

DISCLAIMER:

THIS BOOK IS NOT MEANT AS, NOR DOES IT INTEND TO BE, A SUBSTITUTE FOR PROFESSIONAL PSYCHIATRIC OR PSYCHOTHERAPY SERVICES. NOR IS ANY ADVICE GIVEN MEANT TO BE TAKEN AS PROFESSIONAL TREATMENT BY THE AUTHOR.

Dedicated to You, Your Marriage, and, last but not least, Your Kids

Introduction

A Brand New Collection of Essays

Life is wonderful, at times difficult, and, in my opinion, never boring, especially if you like to occasionally take a look under the hood.

In keeping with the mechanical metaphor, but switching over from cars to bicycles, picture life as a bicycle---The Bicycle of Life---and on that bike there's a Work Wheel and a Love Wheel. The Bicycle of Life is what this book is all about: Growing up into a 'responsible adult', getting married, parenthood, work life, growing up some more. This stuff can be really hard, especially if you're in it for the long haul.

Most of us are trying to do the right thing. It's just that we really don't have a clue or any guidance about how to do it. I aim to provide you with some guidance in this book, along with companionship and support along the way, just as I would if you and I were sitting together in my office.

Of course, I can't tell anybody how to live their lives, what to believe, or how to behave, and this we both know. What I can do, however, is share the things I've found useful, fascinating, and true about living a good life. I can share the knowledge of how to navigate the Work Wheel and the Love Wheel, and my goal is to do just that.

By the way, you don't have to be married or have your own children in order to benefit from this book. You yourself are someone's child, even if you don't have any of your own, so you will gain some insights into your own childhood with this book. You're likely involved in some interpersonal relationships in your life, ranging from friendships to romantic relationships, and possibly even including dealing with nephews and nieces or your friends' and neighbors' kids. You've also got a work life of some sort. And chances are you're trying to balance all of this the best way you can. You qualify.

I'm really proud of this particular book. I took my time with it---five years to be exact. Though most of it was written between 2010 and 2012, I decided to take the next two years to edit it---which essentially turned out to be three years---and I ended up rewriting pretty much the entire thing in the process. This was tough for me as I'm usually not that patient about having to wait to share the work I love so much with others. But, I took a deep breath as well as some of the advice in the book, worked on my Restraint and on my Anxiety Modulation, and somehow found the patience needed.

The result is this real world instruction guide on how to work with yourself to improve the way you live your life. The chapters are really just short essays. Some are based on blog posts I've written over the years, and some are refinements or expansions of topics I've addressed in my first three books. Still others are based entirely on brand new material that I've never had an opportunity to sit down and write about until now.

Using the feedback people have given me from my previous books, I decided to go with the short-essay format from my first book, Cobwebs and Ugly Wallpaper, which consisted of completely independent topics that could be read in any order. This format allowed the reader to always come away with a complete topic in mind and a sense of accomplishment each time he or she sat down to read the book. People liked that. Especially busy people. And I've again kept the subject matter multi-layered---almost allegorical at times---so that the essays could be appreciated and useful from your first read today, to years later when you've read them again from a completely different place in your life.

Is the book substitute for personal, couples, or family therapy? No it's not, and I don't think any book really is. Nor is it intended as such. But I do know lots of people who are either in therapy or who have had some in the past, as well as plenty of others who have no intention of ever stepping foot into a therapist's office. With this book I wanted to appeal to both sorts of folks, much as it was with the Cobwebs book.

Finally, a new feature that I've added to this book is a simple coding system that helps you to choose the chapters you'd like to read about at any given moment, depending on what you're in the mood to read. The way it works is that each chapter has both a title as well as a letter in parenthesis after the title which specifies whether that chapter is about You (Y), Kids (K), or Marriage (M).

This way you will know what chapters you might want to check out based upon what your gut tells you that you need that day. I've also included those code letters in the table of contents at the beginning of the book, so that you can easily skim through the different topics and know exactly what page to turn to in order to read what you want to read.

Well, I guess that's it! The rest is ahead of you and up to you to explore, to learn, and, most of all, to enjoy.

Anthony Ferraioli, M.D.
New York, USA

Chapter 1

How to Live a Peaceful Life (Y)

A friend of mine once asked me to give him a list of the top ten things I've learned in my work about how to live a happy, peaceful life.

Well, narrowing it down to ten is difficult, as people have truly taught me so much over the years, but here goes:

1. Be spiritual, even religious if you wish. Don't be afraid of the "r" word. And don't be too afraid to delve a bit into whatever religion or spirituality you lean towards or that feels right and true to you—maybe it's even the one you were born into! And be consistent so that it has a chance to get into you.

2. Take care of business today. Procrastination is often fueled by fear. Fear of failure, fear of success, fear of imperfection, etc. It also saps away your vital life energy and tranquility, which you could use for other things.

3. Don't seek chaos. It's an unnecessary habit and it ultimately produces unneeded anxiety, confusion, and feelings of being out of sorts and disconnected from yourself. This includes unhealthy relationships and all acting out behaviors such as alcohol and drug abuse, sex addictions, affairs, AND retail therapy.

4. Read. Someone once told me that a person will always be happy as long as they have books to read. These include the ones on your Kindles, Nooks, and iPads! Reading takes us into the minds and hearts of others and it broadens our perspective and our paradigms, all of which helps when life makes us feel anxious, depressed, or afraid.

5. Exercise. You don't have to go overboard. Just do something which lets you feel in touch with your body and your breathing. Being physically in touch with yourself releases neurotransmitters which help with tranquility and healthy self-confidence.

6. Connect with someone every day just to connect. If you have kids, focus on them exclusively for a bit of time on a regular basis without multitasking. You'll know what you've been missing the minute you start doing this.

7. Don't always look for something in the future to focus or rely upon to 'pick you up' or 'pull you through' like a trip, a new possession or relationship, etc. Just practice enjoying the moments you have as well as the things and the relationships you have right now. Spend time and energy nurturing your life and everything in it rather than always living your life for tomorrow and wasting today.

8. Forgive. Someone once told me that family forgives because that's what family does. If you've ever been really angry with someone in your family for offending or disappointing you, you know how difficult this can truly be. (Situations of continued, repeated abuse and violence are more complex and sometimes dangerous and must be addressed as such.)

9. Tolerate. Work on your patience with others and with yourself. We can always say more, prove more, argue more, etc. But in the end, we're all going to the same place and we won't be able to bring our points and our opinions with us.

10. Serve. Doesn't have to be particularly heroic or wide reaching. Serve your spouse. Serve your children. Serve your aging parents. Get used to serving, in any way that you can. It's a good way to remind ourselves that there's a big world out there and that we're not all alone.

AND...for extra credit:

11. Be committed and follow-through. This includes your marriage, your kids, your work, your avocations, and your word. Yes, you can change course when necessary and appropriate but quite often we do this too often and too erratically:

We must not constantly remove the value of things in our lives and make everything disposable if we don't want to live lives which feel meaningless and empty to us.

CHAPTER 2

DEALING WITH CHRONIC FEAR AND WITH ANTICIPATORY ANXIETY (Y)

Are you a person whose life is often dictated by fear and anticipatory anxiety?

Anticipatory anxiety is simply the anxiety we feel when we worry about something that has yet to occur. When chronic, it can be a crippling affliction and many more of us suffer from at least some degree of this than we may care to believe.

Do you avoid going to the doctor for fear of "what might turn up"? Or do you put off certain things as long as possible, hoping that they'll just "go away"?

Do some of life's major decisions, such as those involving health care, money, and family issues seem to never get addressed because of fear or anticipatory anxiety about what can or might happen?

I hear you my friend.

The problem with allowing fear and anticipatory anxiety to rule our lives all the time is that it can get us into trouble.

Sure it's true that most of us feel some fear and anticipatory anxiety sometimes (or maybe more than sometimes); and it's also true that many of us allow it to win the day sometimes. But it is very important to know when it's absolutely necessary not allow it to influence our decisions.

This is very basic, fundamental knowledge that we all need to know and that children need to be taught by example from the adults around them.

Unfortunately for many of us, the adults back in our childhoods also suffered from paralyzing fear and anticipatory anxiety or, at the very least, they proved themselves unable to tolerate our innocent, normal, childhood fears and anxieties back then. This, of course, only made things worse for us as many of us had no healthy adult role models to teach us how to deal with normal fears and anxieties.

Children need adults to help them learn to find their courage.

They already have courage; they just need us to help them find it and support it so that it (and they) can grow healthily.

Once children grow up, it becomes quite difficult to reverse the damage that has been done in terms of the various fears, hypervigilance, and anxieties they find themselves experiencing about the world around them as adults.

What To Do Now: Suspending Fear

What we, as adults, need to do now is to slowly, gradually, and Deliberately learn to reconnect with and support the courage that we once had inside of us as children before it was influenced by the environment, including the adults, around us.

In order to do this, we must practice what I call Suspending Fear.

The spirit of Suspending Fear involves trying to get back to a state when our minds were not yet mapped out with all the fears and anticipatory anxieties that were imprinted on them in childhood and young adulthood.

It is a technique which allows us to Deliberately and, in a very mechanical, calculated way, turn off our hypervigilance for just a moment or two; just enough time to book that doctor's appointment, health maintenance test (colonoscopy anyone?), difficult meeting with a financial counselor, etc.

By practicing Suspending Fear for just a few moments, we allow ourselves to "act" like we would have acted and as who we were before all the influences and traumatic experiences of childhood and early adulthood took over our minds, hearts, and souls.

It is not about talking ourselves out of the fear, or convincing ourselves not to be fearful. It's about temporarily having what the old Zen masters would call "no mind" or perhaps "right mind." In other words, Suspending Fear is not about putting anything at all into the mind to get rid of the fear; it's about emptying the mind entirely for a few moments.

The problem with fear-based emotions and reactions is that they cannot easily be reasoned away.

Oh, you can try.

And you can convince yourself that you are brave and that you are okay, and this may actually work sometimes for some people.

But, for the majority of us, our fears and anticipatory anxieties go back even further than our verbal skills and cognitive processing skills.

Many of these "pre-verbal" traumas have left us in states of chronic, perpetual hypervigilance which are not only unhealthy in and of themselves, but which also distort and disable our abilities to make appropriate, healthy choices in our adult lives.

We therefore sometimes literally need a "clean slate" or "no mind" for a few moments, so that we can think and behave as we would have before the fear and anxiety made their deep grooves in our minds.

Over the years, I have been blessed in my work to get to know literally thousands of people pretty intimately. They have taught me many lessons to remember as a physician, including the dangers of leading a fear-and-anticipatory-anxiety-driven life.

Some of these lessons include:

People die sometimes because they put things off out of fear and anticipatory anxiety.

What was once benign becomes malignant.

What was once elective and routine becomes emergent and more risky.

Options can sometimes narrow and become less desirable with neglect and the passage of time.

What could have once been done on our own terms, now gets done on someone or something else's terms.

In the end, pain comes to us, even though, and sometimes even more so, when we try to run from it.

So practice the Suspending Fear technique and any other technique you come across or can learn from others. Take your time and do what you can, but at the same time try to push yourself too.

Don't hesitate to do some reading on the subject of fear or to get some preliminary exploratory counseling to learn more about your specific fears and how they affect your choices, decisions, and your life in general.

You might be surprised by what you learn!

Chapter 3

You Can't Get 'Past' What You Haven't Been 'Through' (Y)

How do you cope with stress?

How about loss?

I like to group things like stress, loss, worry, fear, trauma and other strong emotional states into the more general term 'pain'.

Keeping that in mind, people often ask me how to 'get over' various things or circumstances in their lives that are causing them pain.

Sometimes they word it differently, as in, "Doc, tell me how to get past this...", or, "How can I put this behind me...."

Now add this to the fact that, in our culture and time in history, we are inundated with phrases like "Man Up!", or, "Deal With It!", as well as, "Bottom Line", and the perennial classic, "Suck It Up!"

Since when did we all become Marines or Navy Seals?!

Even our large corporations have joined in on the mantras, with Nike popularizing the phrase, "Just Do It", and Toyota, "Moving Forward".

Nowadays it seems that if we find ourselves feeling the least bit uncomfortable or conflicted about something difficult in our lives, or, God forbid, feeling emotional pain as I've just described it on the previous page, we immediately look for the 'fix' for it or the 'cure'—while all the while society is fervently telling us to "Suck It Up!"

We doctors are deep into it too and are sometimes just as bad, especially given how little time is spent with patients these days. In fact, I always tell my patients—only half-jokingly—"please don't cry in your primary care doc's office on a Friday; otherwise you'll likely end up on some sort of medication that you and I will be stuck trying to get you off of over the next few months!"

No Cure For Life—And No Real Shortcuts Either

There is no 'cure' for life, as much as we sometimes wish that there were.

The other day I learned that some of the children at a local grammar school were learning a new way to do math.

Though I won't share with you the exact name the technique was given, as I don't want to give away any identifying details of the particular school involved, let's just call it the "make a good guess" technique.

Make a good guess? At seven years old?!?

I don't know about you, but when I was seven there was no such thing as a particularly good guess with what little bit of information and experience my little brain had going for it at the time. (Unless you count guessing cookies vs. brownies for dessert based on the smells emanating from the kitchen!!)

Here's my point: Wow, we start teaching shortcuts early!

Most of us would agree that, later in life, we're often in the position of having to solve or answer something with less than optimal data, so we MUST eventually get good at making an educated 'guestimate'.

But, in my opinion, these children are too soon learning that the fastest way is the best way, and that's just simply NOT always the case.

Especially early on in life, I'd much rather have my kids learn things all the way through the 'long way', before introducing all the shortcuts, because I believe that there is an innate, take-it-with-you-for-the-rest-of-your-life value in the challenge of truly learning something, whether in school or in the school of hard knocks.

The problem is not so much our goal—as a society—to become ever more efficient and effective in our lives; no, the real problem comes when being efficient and effective BECOMES our lives.

And when it comes to experiencing life, especially the hard parts, we really cannot and should not try to rush past it.

It doesn't work anyway. Rushing 'past' is often the best way of ultimately staying stuck.

When we try to rush our minds, bodies, and spirits ahead too quickly, the issues at hand will haunt us forever simply because we've never allowed ourselves to emotionally stick around long enough to sufficiently feel and experience the depths of our situation.

Suck it up, we say to ourselves.

Man up, somebody says to us. Deal with it.

One of the most upsetting things for me to see is when a parent short-circuits an intense emotional experience that his or her child is experiencing in the moment, as in:

"You're okay so stop crying...", or

"Big boys don't cry...", or

"What are you so upset about! You're fine! Stop that right this instant!"

We parents unknowingly model and teach our children how to handle difficult feelings by how we handle the child as they are experiencing them.

If our tolerance for their emotions is low, so it will eventually be, in all likelihood, that their own tolerance for their emotions will also be low. And the cycle will probably continue with their children as well.

If, on the other hand, we lead by example with my LVAC model, where LVAC stands for Listen, Validate, Ask, and Comment (in that order), we will allow the child to truly experience whatever it is that they are feeling or thinking instead of rushing them along.

When we force kids to move along too quickly, it creates what I call 'sticky points', or hang-ups for them later in life, where they perpetually get stuck when they face those same feelings or situations and do not have the tools to negotiate them in a healthy way.

And the same thing goes for us.

The next time you are faced with a difficult or conflictual situation, maybe one that is laden with guilt, shame, fear, or anger, try sharing your feelings with someone or with yourself by writing about them.

Try to 'dwell' for a few moments, or longer if necessary. Don't give yourself short shrift. Stick around for awhile with it.

You can never get 'past' what you haven't been 'through'; it will always come back to haunt you if you try.

So remember, please take care of yourself in a Deliberate, adult manner. Face your pain and work your way through it using all the resources you can pull together—the reason I capitalized the "D" in Deliberate, by the way, is because it is part of my REALADULTS tool where "D" stands for Deliberate, and the first "L" is for LVAC. Tools like this can help you work your way 'through' life, rather than having to try to get 'past' it. More on both of these tools elsewhere in this book.

CHAPTER 4

BEING WHERE YOU'RE SUPPOSED TO BE (Y)

I suppose I could have just as easily called this chapter, 'Doing What You're Supposed To Be Doing'.

People suffer from anxiety. And it's often because they are not doing what they are supposed to be doing. Now, please bear with me for a moment and I'll explain.

The specific kind of anxiety I'm talking about here is what we might call 'free floating' or 'general' anxiety. (Not to be confused with the psychiatric diagnosis of Generalized Anxiety Disorder, or GAD, though there is some overlap here.)

The reason we often feel so 'out of sorts' or generally anxious is that we are disconnected from ourselves.

'Oh boy', you're saying, 'there goes Ferraioli again with the stupid disconnect word.'

Well, sorry, but, you're right, I am talking about that again!

You see, the problem starts when we're very little kids. The adults around us have their own problems; they're distracted, busy, depressed or anxious, self-absorbed, addicted (alcohol, shopping, work, etc.), or whatever else.

They're not particularly in tune with the kids, and certainly not practicing LVAC®. (You might recall that LVAC® is my mnemonic/acronym which stands for Listen, Validate, Ask, Comment.)

What most of us got in childhood was 'reverse-LVAC', in other words, the Comments came first!

Examples of the Comments we got:

"Don't do that!"

"Why did you do that?!" (a Comment disguised as a question)

"Why are you doing that?!"

"Get over here!"

"Don't talk to me like that!"

"Don't talk to your father/mother like that!"

"I said so!"

"You never listen!"

"How many times have I told you...!?"

In addition to various punishments and punitive tones, many people, as children, dealt mostly with the agendas of the adults through their various Comments about the children's behaviors or feelings.

This is where the disconnect begins, which is a lesson to us parents today with regards to our own kids: If you want to promote healthy, whole children with less disconnect within themselves and therefore less anxiety and other problems—learn and practice LVAC® with them!

The process of Listening, Validating, and Asking open-ended questions allows the child finish their full thoughts and feelings within themselves while they are conversing with us.

When we short-circuit this process by Commenting first instead of last, we cause the child to lose their internal emotional bookmark, i.e. where they were going to go with their thoughts and feelings. This is what eventually creates the internal disconnect within themselves which I'll talk more about in a minute.

Children learn about themselves as they're trying to talk to us about things. Short-circuit the one and you also short-circuit the other.

Now, back to our anxiety.

One of the long-term side effects of not getting enough of an LVAC® approach is that disconnect we were talking about a minute ago. Well, guess what?

That disconnect eventually produces a lack of four important things: 1) what we want, 2) what we don't want, 3) what we like, and 4) what we don't like.

If we're disconnected from these fundamental aspects of who we are (in fact, in my practice I call those four things the essence of The True Self), how can we really know what we're supposed to be doing anymore or where we're supposed to be?

You see?

If I'm so disconnected from my internal world that I no longer have a sense of the things I should be doing or not doing, then I will suffer more from free floating anxiety.

Now you say, 'Okay Ferraioli, but I can't exactly go back to my childhood and get any of your "L-VAC" can I now!?'

You're right again!

So here's what we have to do: begin to pay attention to what your instincts are again.

Since childhood created the disconnect, we must use adulthood to reconnect with ourselves by cultivating, in a Deliberate way—like you would do at your job—a sense of who we are again.

Start to listen to the little voice-instinct inside you; the one that says, 'I've got 10 million things to do today, but what I really want to do is XYZ.'

"What I really want to do is XYZ"—that's the voice of your true self. (And no, you can't just do ANYTHING, like break the law or other immoral or unethical things—the goal is to reconnect with who you are again, not to hurt people or yourself.)

This may be hard at first. In fact, it may be very hard indeed.

You may find yourself having to make some difficult decisions. Model airplane club not doing it for you anymore? Drop it and see what grows for you next in its place. Weekly get together with the guys or gals turning into a drag? Let it go and see what comes up in your heart and mind to do instead. Book club draining you? Ask yourself why and if the answer is that it just generally doesn't do it for you, then it must go.

The point of all this is that it will take courage, focus, and a Deliberate attitude to help your disconnect heal.

But once you find out where you're supposed to be and what you're supposed to be doing, whether that means for this moment, for this day, or for the longer term in your life, your anxiety will diminish.

Eventually.

Keep in mind that at first you may actually experience an increase in anxiety because you've spent years—maybe decades—following a beat that was never actually yours to begin with. (Remember all those disconnect-producing Comments that we talked about from childhood that you dealt with and internalized?)

Let's use a quick example.

Say you've woken up on a Saturday morning with tons of things to do and that you're about to go through said list in a robot-like fashion in order to 'get it all done'.

That may be very appropriate in some cases, but let's also say that, upon examining your list and deciding what's absolutely vital (e.g. child care issues, home maintenance, paying bills, health care issues, etc.), you come to some items that are neither vital, nor of particular interest to you or who you really are (i.e. what you like, don't like, want, or don't want). Yes, who you really are actually counts now and we need to make room for it.

Nobody said tackling free floating anxiety would be easy.

Now, if you've decided that some of those items can go, take some time to be with yourself and 'listen' to what you 'hear'. Take the following example.

A friend of mine once told me that, no matter where he was or how packed his schedule seemed to be, he could always narrow down 'one absolute thing' that he wanted to do that day. He would always try to make that thing happen, no matter what, and, he often found that the other, less important things would fit their way in around the 'one thing' anyway.

Life is short.

Let's you and I make sure that, in addition to fulfilling our various, vital obligations in our lives, we also practice tuning in to ourselves to find out what we are supposed to be doing as well.

In other words, let's actually LIVE too, shall we?

All the best in learning these ideas and this approach, and decreased anxiety to you!

CHAPTER 5

FORGIVENESS IN YOUR MARRIAGE (M)

Do you trust your spouse? I guess a better way to ask this question would be: Do you have trust in your spouse?

In order to talk about forgiveness in your marriage, we first have to look at how we lose the trust in each other.

Let's divide trust into two basic categories: "Macro-trust" and "Micro-trust."

Macro-trust is the trust we usually think about when we're talking about trust in a relationship and it covers the big things like fidelity, addictions, violence towards each other, and willingness to discuss issues.

If a marriage doesn't have Macro-trust, generally speaking, it's not a viable relationship and it won't last.

For now I want us to focus on the other kind of trust, namely, Micro-trust.

This trust is the one we don't usually think about very often, at least not deliberately and consciously. It involves things like trusting your spouse to handle whatever it is you need to tell them without making you feel bad or attacking you or ignoring you or getting defensive with you right away.

Micro-trust also involves the feeling of knowing that your spouse will support you emotionally in life, including trying to understand your desires, wishes, what you want, don't want, like, and don't like. It is the knowledge that you have that your spouse truly thinks about you even when you're not around, and even when there's nothing immediately in it for them.

Micro-trust is often the trust we lose first in our marriages. It begins to fade as we "betray" each other with our lack of truly Listening, Validating, Asking questions to learn about each other, and Commenting last, if at all.

We also lose this trust when our spouses begin to sense a childishness about us which often shows itself in our selfishness or even our narcissism, so to speak. It is that vibe we give off that says, "Sure I *love* you, but, hey, I come first when the s@%t hits the fan!" That means that if I'm low energy, tired, hungry, frustrated, distracted, worried, or somehow overwhelmed, I'll snap at you, deprioritize you, become sarcastic with you, not listen to you or try to hear you, etc. And all the while I'll also make demands of you. In a word, I'll be an Emotionally Incompetent Adult with you when I'm under duress, or perhaps any time at all- totally unpredictable!

The problem with losing the Micro-trust is that, unlike Macro-trust issues, it's often insidious. If you have an affair, or spend your paycheck on alcohol or drugs, or gamble it away, it'll be pretty obvious that your spouse won't trust you for long.

But with Micro-trust issues; issues like lack of consideration, lack of listening, a sense of uncaring or inconsistency, the effect is often one of buildup of resentment and disconnect in the marriage.

Now for the forgiveness part.

People will often tell me, once they've learned about these things, that they can literally pinpoint the moments in which they began to lose the Micro-trust in their spouses, or vice-versa: a lie here, an outburst there, a deception or ulterior motive over there. Whatever the case may be, they begin to see what happened.

Now the question becomes, what can we do about it to fix it?

People have taught me that one important step which needs to be addressed before there can be true healing in a marriage is the forgiveness step.

We must literally ask our spouses for forgiveness.

But this goes beyond simply saying, "I'm sorry."

Asking for this kind of forgiveness involves more than just words. It involves a mindset, a spirit, and an adjustment in your heart.

It involves allowing yourself to first feel the pain which led you to act the way you acted or would habitually act with the other person. We often live or act out our pain on other people, and we don't even realize that we're in pain to begin with.

Maybe we're angry, frustrated, afraid, uncertain, confused, anxious, excited, worried, or out of sorts somehow. The fact is that we acted out this "pain" on the other person, and most likely more than once.

So when we're contemplating asking for forgiveness, we must first take ownership of our true feelings. This way, the act of asking for forgiveness actually starts with addressing ourselves first; our pain.

Next, we think about the pain, confusion, betrayal, anger, sadness, or despair we've caused the other person. We must feel some of that as well, for we are responsible for that too.

In other words, asking for forgiveness in a truly adult, Emotionally Competent way means that we are acknowledging both our own pain, as well as the pain we've caused the other person.

Now this process may take you some time to go through so don't rush it or it won't be as real as it needs to be. When you ask for forgiveness in the way that I'm describing, you are also asking, begging actually, for a clean slate. You see, we humans usually don't like to think of ourselves as being disliked or as being the source of someone's pain; it simply discourages us from being able to change the things in ourselves that we need to change.

No, in order to truly and permanently change and grow into our most Emotionally Competent, true adult selves, it is vital that we feel forgiven by those we've hurt the most.

And, especially in our marriages, this becomes an essential prerequisite to the process of rebuilding the Emotional Credibility with each other that we've lost over the years when we lost the Micro-trust. Remember, Emotional Credibility=trust+liking the other person and wanting to be around them.

CHAPTER 6

AN LVAC PRIMER (K)

Over the past several years, much has been written, talked about, and practiced with regards to my LVAC™ acronym/mnemonic, so I wanted to step back and take a moment and review what LVAC really means and where it came from.

Before we begin, let me tell you what LVAC stands for: "L" is for Listen, "V" is for Validate, "A" is for Ask, and "C" is for Comment—in that order.

Here's a secret: Years ago, after a busy few months at my psychotherapy office, I sat down in front of an empty sheet of lined paper with the intention of writing down my idea of the perfect father.

Now, I don't recall, nor can I tell you presently, why I was so specific back then about wanting to define father rather than mother or parents in general.

I can only say that it was probably a combination of my professional work and development at the time as well as my own new role as a father myself back then.

(Of course, I also had that uncanny and universal qualification we all have of having once been a young child with parents of my own.)

And so it was that, when I sat down in front of that empty sheet of paper, what I wanted to find out was how to be an ideal father, and, to some extent, an ideal therapist as well.

You might be sitting there, shaking your head, saying, "Umm..a therapist is NOT somebody's father and nor is a physician....AND what about your patients/clients who are older than you are? You're certainly not their father or father figure!"

It's true.

I can only say in return that, whenever we humans look to someone for support or to help us with our pain, part of what we need to do is to be able to trust them and respect them. Age is not a factor here. I've at times figuratively been 'father' to seventy and eighty year olds almost as much as I've literally been a father to my children. Sometimes I'm also their brother, their son, their 'spouse', or their friend.

And what's important about inventing LVAC is that I wanted to know something fundamental and true:

What is the basic, universal thing that we humans, all of us, really need and thrive on?

Is it money?

Is it attention?

Food?

Sex?

No, what people have taught me is this:

The fundamental, basic need we humans all have is the need to be heard.

In serving thousands of people, first for a brief time in primary care, then in psychiatry, I've learned that we human beings really want and need to be heard.

We don't want to necessarily argue, yet again.

We don't want to 'stir the pot' or 'be a problem'.

We want to be heard, and we also want to be understood; if not by someone else, then at least by ourselves.

And what about Listening?

We may not have been born being good at Listening (the "L" in LVAC), but we were born to be heard.

Listening first, instead of Commenting first, is something we must train ourselves to do.

Think about it.

A baby is born and we celebrate in the delivery room when he or she does what...?

Cries!

But, surely, you might ask, as we grow up into true, Emotionally Competent adults, we must do more than simply crave being heard all the time, right?

Correct.

What we must do, if our goal is to grow as Emotionally Competent individuals, is to cultivate the art of Listening, which is the first step of the LVAC approach.

Next, we must learn to Validate the other person's feelings and thoughts.

We don't have to necessarily agree with them, but we do need to Validate before we Comment with our own opinion or agenda.

It's just a fact of nature.

If it's an adult we're dealing with, then Validating them avoids triggering all of their defenses and allows for greater closeness and understanding in our communication with them.

And, as is the subject of this post, if it's a child we're dealing with, then it becomes vital to LVAC, and here's why:

The effect of Listening, Validating, Asking open-ended questions, then Commenting last, if at all, allows the child to stay emotionally connected with us and with themselves and it reinforces their sense of self and their core mental and emotional health.

It allows them to grow healthy inside. In fact, it would put me out of business as they all grew up into happy, thriving, well-adjusted adults with minimal residual hurts and pain from childhood, having been heard and validated by the most important people in their lives, we, their parents.

Instead, when we Comment first, which can be with our words or with our behaviors (e.g. rolling our eyes, getting up from the table and leaving, etc.), we express our agenda to them and we short-circuit their development:

"Dad, I'm going to try this new sport."

"Oh, I don't know; I think it's dangerous." (that's a Comment and it's my agenda, i.e. anxiety/worry) vs.:

"Dad, I'm going to try this new sport."

"Oh, cool. What's it involve?" (that's Validating + Asking and it's about their agenda—good!)

The natural fact is—and I didn't make it up or put it there—that we humans grow to trust and to like and respect those who LVAC with us.

We rely on them.

We go to them with our problems, hurts, and fears, no matter how old we or they are.

We trust them.

We feed off of them and grow because of them.

And, as you may know from prior chapters: trust + likability=Emotional Credibility.

So, when you LVAC, two things are happening:

1) you are helping the other person heal, thrive, and become more solid at their core

and

2) you are earning Emotional Credibility points with them

When we do this with our spouses, we get all sorts of benefits and healing in the relationship.

So, is there ever a time for Commenting?

Why yes, of course.

BUT, unless it's some sort of dire emergency or instructional course that you're trying to teach (like a language for instance), you should only Comment after you've really learned about what the other person is feeling and trying to say—and therefore after you've also given them the gift of allowing them to learn more about themselves at the same time.

You will meet with much less defensiveness in your life in general, and, as a parent, you will be giving your child the equivalent of emotional diamonds, if you understand and practice LVAC.

CHAPTER 7

CHRONIC ANGER (Y)

Are you chronically angry?

Or does someone you are close to always seem angry, frustrated, or upset?

There are reasons why we humans can be like this, including but not limited to high levels of stress, health problems, and, for many, old childhood emotional wounds and injustices which haven't yet healed.

For that last one, the emotions can often be quite complex-- some combination of anger plus fear plus humiliation or shame, for example. And if you combine all these you get rage.

In fact, I would argue that many of those who appear to be chronically angry are really suffering from old childhood wounds and injustices which are probably unconscious to them.

What they do with all that pain, however, is often very noticeable in the conscious day-to-day realm and often quite destructive to their relationships, including with their children and their spouses.

What chronic anger can look like varies with each person, but it can include:

-being short with people

-yelling

-being cold or withdrawn

-constantly being sarcastic or joking at other peoples' expense

-always being defensive or negative

-being contentious or contrarian

-appearing to be or being thought of as a 'miserable person'

-being vengeful or quick to hold grudges

-chronically sabotaging others (or oneself)

-assuming the worst about others or about a given situation

Other, less obvious, but nonetheless significant examples of chronic anger, resentment, and frustration include (some of these may surprise you as you may not see the immediate connection with anger):

-chronic forgetfulness in an otherwise healthy individual

-tuning people out (or certain people) and not 'hearing' them

-chronic lack of follow through or lack of caring or taking things seriously when needed

-chronic 'tiredness' or 'doom and gloom' in an otherwise healthy individual (unexpressed anger or anger turned inwards and 'imploding' on the Self can cause or contribute to both depression and chronic fatigue)

-chronic boredom or disconnect

Bottom line: it's important to know that most people who are chronically angry are in pain. They seem miserable and behave the way they do because they don't know how to escape from the emotional chains that bind them.

Maybe they were given too much responsibility too early on by their parents or by the circumstances of their childhoods. Maybe they were abused. Or maybe they had other great losses that we can only imagine.

So unless they are breaking the law or acting out physically towards others or self-destructively, we really need to start with an empathetic approach when dealing with them. (By the way, empathy is not the same as weakness.)

An empathetic approach includes both trying to understand the other person—as well as—setting appropriate limits and boundaries with them when necessary. This way we help them both heal and grow, and at the same time we do not allow ourselves to be further compromised or hurt by their destructive behaviors.

Every chronically angry person—unless they are a sociopath without guilt or compassion, (i.e. a conscience), or unless they have a major psychotic disorder, (e.g. schizophrenia, delusional disorder, etc.), where their ability to understand reality is by definition compromised—has a healthy part of themselves that knows on some level that they are doing something wrong when they act out in an angry manner.

They are, in fact, either consciously or subconsciously looking for someone to help them STOP.

When we set boundaries with them, without anger or contempt, we are appealing to their healthier side; the side of them which 'gets it' and which agrees with us on some level and wants to grow and to heal.

Of course, if the person, in addition to being chronically angry, is psychotic, as I've mentioned, or is somehow dangerous to you or to others, professional help is required.

What if YOU are the one who is chronically angry?

My first piece of advice is to focus extra hard on practicing and honing one of my adult skills, namely, Restraint.

This skill is also known in my office as the 'bite the tongue technique'.

You must convince yourself that much of what you say, and, in fact, that many of your first impulses and reactions, are really about YOU and your past traumas, like all those hurts and injustices from your childhood and years past that I mentioned before.

You must learn to not trust these first impulses and reactions enough to immediately act on them anymore, for they are destructive to your life and relationships today.

In other words, practice Restraint.

On a practical level, this entails keeping most of your Comments to yourself and, instead, practicing my LVAC technique by Listening, Validating others, Asking open-ended questions, and Commenting last, if at all. Your Comments are where your anger is hidden, and others will notice whether you do or not.

Practice hard, like you would any other skill, and it WILL pay off handsomely in your healing process. You will find yourself growing and getting stronger, and you will find your Emotional Credibility (trust + likability) skyrocketing with others.

Though we must respect where these strong feelings and reactions came from and what they represent to us and to our life's story, we must also learn to train ourselves to no longer allow these feelings and reactions to dictate our behavior or to control us and our lives.

Let's help free you from the demons of the past which keep you trapped inside the angry, false shell of your true self.

Sometimes people need professional help getting there and that's perfectly fine. Sometimes counseling and even a bit of medication will help you get started if you can't yet do it by yourself.

What's important is that you learn a better way to take care of yourself and your pain.

There are REASONS why you always feel angry, frustrated, overwhelmed, threatened, or scared. Don't let your life go by and your relationships suffer without addressing them, and yourself, properly and with care.

CHAPTER 8

CREATING HAPPY MEMORIES (K)

How will your kids remember you?

A morbid question, I know.

And how about your spouse, if he or she outlives you?

Are you mainly the disciplinarian in your house? Or are you the 'good time Charlie'?

Does your spouse see you as an angry or miserable person most of the time?

Do you tend to always be nervous or worried about what needs to be done next, or what has yet to be done?

Are you rarely ever PRESENT and FOCUSED in the moment with your family?

Do you think that you 'add to' or 'take away from' the overall milieu at home?

Life is short.

Before we know it our kids are grown and don't need us quite as much and in the same ways they used to; and when we look in the mirror we start to see our mothers and fathers.

I think it's important, during these times of ever increasing freneticism in our lives, to consider how quickly time goes by and how quickly opportunities to record happy memories go by with it.

When is the last time you were with your children and DIDN'T feel an internal pressure to be elsewhere or to be doing something else?

Are you a constant multi-tasker? Or do you have times when you consciously and deliberately switch gears so that you can focus on one thing at a time and give yourself a break?

Are you always trying to "get through" your day or do you sometimes actually get to "live" your day in a deliberate, conscious, and enjoyable manner?

Have you ever experimented with just answering "yes" to your kids requests to do things with them, just to see where they'll lead you?

Examples:

"Mommy, can you color with me?"

"Daddy, can you come outside and play with me?"

"Mommy, can we bake something together?"

"Daddy, can you come help me with this?"

How quick are you to say "no" to them or "in a minute!"? How about to your spouse?

Saying "yes" can sometimes help us push our limits when our old patterns and mental grooves tell us that we can't, shouldn't, couldn't, wouldn't, mustn't, or dare not!

(I quite recently found my early-middle-aged-self sliding down a dry mountain on my early-middle-aged-butt, sitting inside a way-too-small rubber tube wondering if my disability insurance was all paid up! I'm sure my kids --and my wife-- will remember that one for quite some time!)

One of the reasons I so enjoy treating adults in my practice who happen to also be parents is that they already come with a built-in mechanism for self-growth: their kids!

Kids are forever pushing us to be what they need us to be, and I absolutely love that fact.

Now if only we'd take their lead and go for it!

I think that part of our task in life, other than to simply survive, is to find ways to flourish and to grow into relatively competent, calm, secure adults. In other words, it's not just about survival, it's also about growth.

Life doesn't give us all the answers, no matter how old we become, but it DOES give us plenty of opportunities to learn, and it also constantly invites us to jump up to the next plateau and take it from there.

For many of us, childhood experiences with our original caregivers did not give us the model or framework we would have needed in order to be able to see ourselves mastering life and thriving. We may have been shown how to 'handle' life, but not necessarily how to conduct it masterfully and with a sense of adventure and grace.

Survival, yes.

Mastery, tranquility, and extra 'emotional fat on the bone'?

No.

So let's practice pushing ourselves and broadening our abilities in our lives.

If you're already married and have children, you've got your built-in laboratory right there! Practice saying "yes" to your family more and more and see where it takes you for the day.

You might be surprised where you find yourself (on a mountain top with a few extra heart beats?), and what you find yourself doing!

And, you'll be grabbing life, stopping that unstoppable clock for a moment or two, and creating some permanent, happy memories!

CHAPTER 9

DO YOU TREAT YOUR SPOUSE AS YOU WOULD WANT YOUR CHILD TO BE TREATED BY THEIRS? (M)

What?!?

A complicated question at first sight, right?

But think about it: If you are a parent like me, do you ever worry about how your child's spouse will treat them?

I know I do.

I think we ALL worry about these things; at least if we're being honest with ourselves.

Most of us would agree that the love we have for our children is the purest form of unconditional love we've ever felt for another human being, and that we would wish nothing more than for them to always be safe and happy.

As I point out in my book, Don't Get Married! (Unless You Understand A Few Things First), unconditional love is different from what I call the "unconditional positive regard" that we have for our spouses.

Unconditional positive regard is a term I coined that means 'benefit of the doubt', or, 'innocent before proven guilty', and it represents the best we can strive for in our marriages if we hope to build a solid, trusting foundation with our spouses.

But it is NOT unconditional love.

The reason there is a difference between the unconditional love we have for our children and the unconditional positive regard we can work towards with our spouses is simply because, when it comes to peer-to-peer relationships (like that between spouses), we expect something IN RETURN from them; that is, we expect THEIR unconditional positive regard for us too!

With spouses, it's a two-way street. We are peers. We give, but they must give too. Nothing's completely for free. That's unconditional positive regard, but not unconditional love.

With children, it's different, especially while they're still young, say, under thirty or so. With them, we give because we OWE them—we're the ones who chose to have them and to put them here on Earth. They did not ask to be born. At the very least and for that reason alone, we owe them our unconditional love.

And that is how I conceptualize the difference.

We parents are the ones who are SUPPOSED to give unconditional love to our children. No one else will. There will always be conditions, no matter how subtle or obvious. Once they grow up, they can only hope for the nearest approximation from their spouses, unconditional positive regard; that is, if they and their future spouses work on it.

But if you're like me, you wish your kids could ALWAYS get unconditional love; and that they'll always be safe and happy and engaged with their lives even after we are gone.

When you picture the way your child might be treated by a future spouse, how do you imagine or hope it looks like?

I know that some time ago, my parents-in-law had to entrust their 'little girl' to me in marriage, and that my own folks had to make a similar adjustment regarding their 'little boy' as well.

They hoped for the best for their respective children in marriage. That's just the way parents think.

This perspective never really changes for parents, at least not the ones I've talked to. And I don't think it will ever change for me either. Our kids will always be our kids, no matter how old they—or we—become.

I want my son or daughter-in-law to give me the same feeling I try to give my parents-in-law: that their child is safe and can thrive and grow with me; that I will continue to work on my flaws and to grow in my Emotional Competence. I too want to know that my children are safe, happy, and thriving and growing with their spouses.

So, again, from the beginning:

Do you treat your spouse as you would want your child to be treated by theirs?

Yes or no?

Is there a tenderness and a respect there?

Is there loyalty, compassion, fidelity?

If (when) you make mistakes, do you try to correct them, learn, and grow from them?

Are you always striving to become a more Emotionally Competent, true adult?

Is there support, no matter how you feel about what your spouse is doing or what they are asking of you? Do you give them the benefit of the doubt, (unconditional positive regard), so that you could respectfully discuss differences in opinion?

Are you trustworthy with your spouse's heart? I call this trust 'Micro-Trust' in my marriage book. It means trusting someone with your feelings; that they will Listen to you and Validate you before making their own Comments. It also means that they will use and practice Restraint.

It is a goal of parenting to Listen, Validate, and Ask first, then Comment last to our children. I call this technique LVAC™ and it works.

Why shouldn't we do LVAC with our spouses?

In fact, why shouldn't we try to treat our spouses as somebody else's child; one who was cherished and precious at one time, or at least should have been?

Why shouldn't they be the apple of our eye?

In the end, if and when your children choose to marry, it will all come together, you'll see.

What I mean here is multigenerational in nature: that the person they choose will treat them as they have become USED to being treated by you; and that you WILL have an emotional reaction to seeing how they are being treated by that person.

Let us hope, for all our sakes as parents, that we LIKE who they pick and what we see.

I don't know about you, but this inevitability motivates me to do my best with both my spouse and my children every day.

The goal is NOT to never mess it up; that's impossible. The goal is to at least know something about what is going on so that you can work on it and improve your skills continuously.

Your spouse deserves this.

Your kids deserve this.

You deserve this.

CHAPTER 10

DO YOU DO FREE TIME? (Y)

Do you DO free time?

When we were kids, we all pretty much knew how to DO free time, didn't we? We knew how to 'hang out'.

But, then, as we grew up and were 'trained', first in school then in our work lives either inside or outside the home, we learned to keep busy and goal-oriented.

Goal-oriented. Hmm...

This term often comes up in psychiatry referring to a person's thinking patterns and behaviors. Are they 'goal-oriented'? Or not so much....

Oh...kay....

Well, what if we relearned to NOT be so goal-oriented all the time?

How would this change our lives? Would it increase quality of life?

For you and me, I absolutely think it would, and here's why:

If we are to try to build the fundamental 'bonds of relationship' with other people, as well as within ourselves, I believe that we need to allow a certain amount of unstructured, non-goal-directed time.

I really believe that.

We must spend TIME. No way around it. Can't make it 'efficient' or easier or more streamlined.

Building the 'bonds of relationship' requires time.

We need to re-learn how to just hang out.

Now, don't get me wrong, I think it's absolutely fantastic how our children (and we) have learned to accomplish SO much in our lives so quickly.

I, for example, run a private practice, serve the community at a clinic, am an expert witness in court regularly, write a popular blog, write books, am helping raise two children, and am partially responsible for several different species of animals in our zoo, I mean our home.

And I'm sure that you have your list as well.

The question is, can you and I learn to temporarily stop all of this goal-directed activity once in a while and find some peace in being able to just hang out with our kids, our spouses, our friends and neighbors, OR even our animals?

Now I'm talking open, unstructured, free time here.

Because I believe that this kind of time is what helps feed the soul, that it's what feeds our relationships and helps build them; can't be done without it.

Many couples have come into my office feeling distant and disconnected from one another.

After some time, after they've learned to communicate with each other in more productive and less destructive ways, sometimes they're still feeling somewhat distant.

This is an example of where the idea of DOING free time together comes in.

Couples actually need to spend some unstructured, free time with each other in order to allow for growth to occur in their relationships.

We need to get back to being able to just hang out with one another.

To observe each other.

To hear each other.

To learn from and about each other.

And to be friends with one another.

In the movie 'RV', starring Robin Williams, the main character's wife tries to explain to another couple how it seems that in marriage, things start out so exciting and wonderful but end up with the spouses becoming 'partners in the business of life'.

Interestingly enough, the couple she is talking to lives in a Partridge Family style bus and travels the country year round in a VERY freeform way. Needless to say, they do not identify at all with what she's talking about. They spend LOTS of time hanging out together.

But WE do, don't we?

Take a moment to consider HOW you spend time with your family, as well as perhaps with your friends and neighbors.

Are you always pretty much in Drive?

Or do you sometimes actually Park and stay a while?

If the answers to the above are 'yes' and 'no', respectively, then please seriously consider practicing how to DO some free time.

CHAPTER 11

A TIME TO TALK (K)

In this world filled with disconnect, where are our kids supposed to learn how to talk about things?

I propose that moms and dads make it a point in their heads and in their hearts to take a few moments here and there to regularly have conversations with their kids, and NOT just when something's wrong.

You may be uncomfortable with this at first, or maybe a bit confused as to why it's important and how to proceed with it, as you may have never have had this behavior modeled for you when you were a child.

Chances are that not many, or maybe none, of the adults in your childhood ever thought to make the deliberate decision to have regular conversations with you. So I'm going to show you how to do it very simply and effectively. But first: why it's an important thing to do.

By the time we reach adulthood, many of our patterns of thought, emotion, and communication have already been set. Think of these patterns as 'grooves' in the brain.

In adulthood it is quite difficult to change these grooves appreciably since they were formed by the patterns and events of our childhood years.

So, for example, if, in your family of origin, sharing and talking about emotions or thoughts was not encouraged or even discouraged, you will have grown up with a deep groove that makes you tend towards keeping these things to yourself. Maybe talking about situations in your life doesn't even occur to you, or, if it does, maybe you shut down or become paralyzed or upset by any sort of gentle confrontation or challenge.

This personality trait would very likely then play a role, sometimes in very subtle and non-obvious ways, in influencing who you ultimately choose to marry and how you raise your own kids. For example, perhaps you might subconsciously choose a spouse who cannot tolerate you talking about your emotions or who cannot tolerate times when you are not 'strong'; and you would choose them because you are so used to that sort of treatment from your childhood environment. In other words, it's comfortable for you and it's what you're used to so you choose it, even though it's not necessarily healthy for you.

The problem with this trait is that it cuts you off from connecting properly with your spouse, your kids, and even yourself--but because that's all you know, that's what you will do and that's what you will model for your kids.

Side effects from all this disconnect can then show themselves as—or worsen—various acting out behaviors such as addictions and escapism, as well as worsen or help cause mood swings, severe depression, and anxiety, among other things.

Now let me share with you a very simple, very powerful technique you can use when you choose to deliberately spend a few minutes having a conversation with your child, thereby teaching them how to be emotionally intimate and connected with you and within themselves.

It goes like this:

First of all, ASK QUESTIONS.

Here's the immediately wonderful thing about this: YOU don't have to know what to say or where to begin!

And make at least some of your questions open ended. By open ended I mean conversation starters/stimulators as opposed to conversation enders:

'So, how's it going?'

'What's up?'

'Tell me about your day today.' (not technically a question, but an open-ended request nonetheless)

Then listen.

Maybe ask some follow up questions.

And by all means, validate the kid's thoughts and emotions instead of immediately contradicting them or becoming defensive or challenging.

Just remember to save your comments for last, if you need them at all.

(By now, you've probably gathered that I just described the LVAC Technique above. But don't worry, LVAC is used throughout this book, so just flip around, continue to read, and you'll learn all you ever wanted to know about it by the time you're through!)

CHAPTER 12

IDEALIZATION AND DISAPPOINTMENT IN DATING AND MARRIAGE (M)

When we are with someone for a long enough period of time, we go from an initial 'idealization' phase in which they can do no wrong, to an eventual 'devalue' phase in which they disappoint us, leading to resentment and disconnect.

Remember that feeling you had when you were first going out with or dating your spouse?

You couldn't get enough of them. You probably spent hours with them or talking on the phone with them.

You thought about them and just the thought of them made you feel good and warm inside.

You not only viewed the world through your eyes, but through their eyes as well: "Sally would love this", you would say or think, or, "Johnny would hate that".

This is only natural.

Some people call it the butterflies stage, or perhaps the honeymoon stage.

I call it the 'idealization phase' of the relationship.

Many people call it being 'in love'.

These stages in a relationship are universal and mostly predictable. But they are also a major contributor to marital discord, misery, and eventual acting out behaviors which can lead, in many cases, to divorce.

What we need to do is to begin to learn how to go from the 'in love' or 'idealization phase' of our relationships, through the 'devalue' phase, and onwards to the real work of getting to actually know the person we are with.

Not very romantic, I realize. But VERY real.

And it works.

We need to view marriage (as described in my marriage book), as an Emotional Laboratory where the main object of exploration is ourselves. Again, not the most romantic interpretation of what marriage is, but, also again, this model really does work in real life.

Take a look: First we date someone, then we 'choose' them somehow, then maybe we marry them.

Then the problems begin, if they haven't already surfaced before the wedding.

But there is a WEALTH of information about ourselves here.

Why did we choose them?

What do they do that disappoints us?

What are our expectations of them?

What are our expectations of our lives? Of ourselves?

How do we handle disappointment? Hurt? Anger? Fear?

Sadness, despair, loss?

You can see why marital and other long-term intimate relationships are Emotional Laboratories for self-exploration.

There's a simple reason why this is so; in other words why marriage and other long-term intimate relationships are unlike any other relationships we'll ever have in our lives.

And that's because our spouses occupy the same spotlight on the stage of our emotional lives as our parents once did.

Whoa! Let me say that again:

Our spouses occupy the same spotlight on the stage of our emotional lives as our parents once did.

That means we have different subconscious expectations of our spouses than we do other people—ones that we often don't fully know about or understand consciously. We hold them to a higher, sometimes impossible standard, at least subconsciously.

And 'subconsciously' is exactly the way we often react towards them. In fact, it's the subconscious, unknown stuff which actually fuels our strong reactions and behaviors towards them in the first place and which sets the stage for the whole idealization vs. devalue phases I talked about earlier.

In other words, since my spouse occupies the same emotional spot in my life as my parents once did, she will inherent all of my resentments, disappointments, childhood rages, feelings of betrayal and injustice, etc., that I have stored away from my childhood when I had no real power or control in that all important parent-child relationship where these things may have originally occurred.

So when she and I marry and I finally have some 'adult' power and sway in this other, adult version of the all important relationship, I can finally act out some of these strong subconscious feelings towards my parental stand in; i.e. my spouse.

Not healthy.

In fact, all our spouses need to do is to push the same buttons that were formed in our earlier, childhood relationships with our parents and, BINGO!, we're off to the races!

Perhaps it's the shame button.

Or maybe the control button.

Or the guilt button, the blame button, the punitive, unfair button. Or the 'I don't like you and never have' button! (Yes, children can sense when we parents don't like them because they're being a 'pain' or are somehow inconvenient for us at the moment.)

SO, back to the 'idealization' and 'devalue' phases.

As I mentioned, the eventual goal is to go through these phases, and to get to a place with each other where we are actively working on getting to know each other for real. Not as each other's parents or children, but as peers, as true adults.

Firstly, the way we begin to do this is by behaving ourselves with each other.

Simple.

Yes, we actually have to behave ourselves in our relationships.

That means Listening to the other person, before Commenting, two steps from my LVAC™ mnemonic which stands for Listen, Validate, Ask, and Comment last.

It means not interrupting them when they are speaking to us.

It means thinking about them even when we don't want something immediately in return from them.

And it means really, truly caring about them, not as a psychological replacement for an emotionally less-than-competent parent, but as somebody else's messed up, hurt child.

That's right, and as I've often said, we are all just somebody's messed up kid, so let's work on having more empathy for one another and let's also look at what we're expecting from each other and whether or not it is reasonable for one peer to be asking it of another.

Let's use Restraint, one of my ten major Adult Emotional Competence skills, along with Anger Modulation, and Anxiety Modulation.

Let's work on Engagement in our lives (another skill) so that we don't expect happiness from our spouses but from ourselves. Marriage is not a cure for loneliness or for an unhappy life.

Let's also practice and learn more about identifying and feeling our pain, rather than acting out our pain towards each other all the time.

And, finally, let's not forget to say, "Thank You", and, "I'm Sorry", when called for (two more skills).

Remember, it's pretty common to idealize someone, then, eventually, to become disappointed and to devalue them. That's not the real problem.

The problem is when we don't understand this is happening and when we don't know what we can do about it, which prevents us from getting through these phases and taking our relationships to the next, more mature and more real, level.

Chapter 13

YOU Are First (Y)

How does the statement, "YOU are first" strike you?

Some people can become very excited and turned on by such a declaration; others can feel anxious, confused, or even afraid, as they find themselves seeking refuge from the spotlight.

With so much going on in the world, in our nation, in our communities, and in our own families, the phrase, "YOU are first", has the potential to become even more daunting.

And in an era when the word Change has become so loaded with political and moral connotations, let me ask you this question:

Just WHO is supposed to change?

How many of us feel that if only that special "something" would occur or come to be we would finally feel better and all would finally be good in our world?

If only our spouse would apologize or understand us better…

If only our children would listen…

If only our jobs were more exciting OR less…

If only we had more free time or more time off…

If only we had more money or felt more loved…

If only we were better understood and appreciated…

If only we were better looking or in better shape or healthier…

If only the weekend would get here already…

If only vacation would get here already…

If only retirement would get here already…

Well, you get the point, which brings us back to my question:

WHO is supposed to change?

I submit to you my friends, that before we squander away our limited time on Earth with all of the if only's of life, what needs to change first is US. We are the ones who need to change.

And with that, let me share two important ideas with you.

Important Idea Number One: Let It Go

Would you, if you were being completely honest with yourself, describe yourself as "sensitive" or "defensive" or "a grudge holder"?

Both my professional and personal experience tells me that this aspect of our personalities can cost us much of our time and emotional energy.

People will ALWAYS hurt us somehow or another, or they will at the very least step on our toes a bit or disappoint us.

That's what happens when we humans try to share space and time with each other.

We need to learn to deal with the messiness of human interaction and cohabitation without letting it paralyze us with chronic anger, resentment, or humiliation, among other things.

In other words, we need to learn to Let It Go.

In my own personal estimation, when somebody has done something to hurt me I find it best to allow for one of three possibilities to help me Let It Go:

1) they apologize and are sorry

2) I learn more about them and try to understand their circumstances, or,

3) I take a blind leap of Faith and Let It Go

If you try this, you'll find that, after a while, you tend to become a bit less sensitive or defensive in your life. And with this change comes better enjoyment of and participation with others.

If I had a nickel for every person who's told me that they'd be better off living in a cabin in the woods, I'd be a rich man.

The reason people feel this way so often is twofold: first, they are afraid of getting hurt, and, second, they are afraid of hurting others.

Instead of moving to the woods, let's learn to Let It Go, so we can actually tolerate and even enjoy one another again.

Important Idea Number Two: (Re)learning How to Play

Another example of what comes up when "YOU are first" is the task of gauging your ability to play in your life.

Neuroscientists have spent decades trying to separate out the right and left brain in terms of functionality.

One of my favorite theories is the one that says that the left brain is where more of our organized, planning, and linear-logical selves live, whereas the right brain houses our spatial and spontaneous selves, as well as our rhythm.

Rhythm, you say?

Yes.

In order to have some fun in our lives, we have to find our rhythm again: it's a right brain concept, a flavor, if you will.

Young children have rhythm.

They know how to play.

They are, in the nonsexual sense of the word, romantic little creatures with plenty of fantasy and imagination.

They are not yet ashamed, or bombarding themselves with myriad norms, inhibitions, rules, and regulations.

Left brain: rules, words, language, logic.

Right brain: big picture, gist, "gets it", feeling.

Most children tend to be VERY right brained, until school and we adults teach them to be more left brained.

Once we grow into adults we are plenty left-brained. Problem is, we've often lost our rhythm in the conditioning process.

It's a funny thing that psychoactive substances like alcohol are often described as mood altering. Because they also tend to disinhibit us.

Why do so many people find pleasure in being intoxicated?

You can bet, at least for some, that it involves feeling less inhibited, more spontaneous, less anxious, less afraid, and less ashamed.

We need to pursue healthful activities and relationships in our lives which help us find our rhythm again.

Bonding with friends or family can do it.

Physical or creative activities, such as sports and the arts, respectively, can do it.

We need to work on taking ourselves less seriously once in a while, feeling less ashamed or embarrassed and less afraid of "goofing up". We need more mutual and unconditional acceptance. And we need the courage and the faith required to put our truest selves out there for the world to see, to deal with, and to appreciate.

Now Do It!

The only thing left to do now that we understand that WE are first, is to go out and Do It!

Start with yourself.

For starters, make it your goal to grow into the best adult you can be by learning how to handle yourself no matter what other people throw at you or what they are up to, by using your awe-inspiring ability to Let It Go.

Then, pursue activities and relationships which allow, indeed promote(!), your ability to play.

Start with these two ideas and you'll soon be on your way to enjoying your life much more, along with the people and circumstances that are part of it.

Chapter 14

Emotional Credibility (Y)

You know that feeling you get when you have a person you can tell anything to, knowing that they won't judge you, or try to correct you, or immediately tell you what they would do or would have done?

You tend to trust that person and you also tend to like having them around you.

Well, if we combine those two elements, i.e. trust + likability, we get what I call Emotional Credibility.

When a person Listens to and Validates our feelings, and maybe Asks an open-ended question or two instead of Commenting right away, we naturally begin to trust them more and they become a valuable resource for us. We also like having them around. This is especially true if we are talking about how a child might feel about a parent, or the way one spouse might feel about the other.

When you walk into a room, do your spouse and children seem to like having you around? Or do they find reasons to 'skeddadle' away from you?

When they think of you, are their first thoughts, "oh, no" or "bummer" or "here comes that negative, miserable person"—or do they think, "hey!" or "optimist" or "I feel good when you are here"?

Do you give off the impression that you know how to live life? Or do you come across as always the victim or malcontent or that life's always too much for you?

If we want to build our Emotional Credibility with the people in our lives, we need to act like emotionally mature adults.

This means doing a few things: being less impulsive or compulsive, less self-centered, less childlike and unable to delay gratification, less negative or miserable, and being MORE competent and in command of ourselves.

If you do a nice thing for your spouse but then become upset while doing it or at the lack of an immediate acknowledgement or thank you, you will have a NET LOSS of Emotional Credibility Points ("E.C. Points" for short)

If you fail to show up at an important family event or appointment with your spouse or to offer your support and follow up for something they are going through, again, you will have a NET LOSS of E.C. Points.

If, on the other hand, you take charge and appear committed and interested in your spouse, your children, or your household chores, you will GAIN E.C. Points.

If you seek to improve your spontaneity, zest for and mastery of your life, creativity and energy for family events or friendships, you will GAIN E.C. Points.

Using LVAC is one foolproof way to improve your Emotional Credibility, as you've probably already gathered from reading about LVAC in another chapter.

There are nine other adult skills you will need to work on and try to master in order to grow into your own best emotionally competent adult self and to break your own E.C. Points record!

These skills form my R.E.A.L.A.D.U.L.T.S. acronym and are scattered throughout this book. They are: Restraint, Engagement in life, Anger modulation, Living with pain and failure (instead of acting it out), Anxiety modulation, Deliberate living, Unconditional positive regard, LVAC, Thank you and I'm sorry, and, finally, Stopping.

Chapter 15

Is Your Spouse a Stranger or "Family" (M)

What happens when we lose the bits of formality and politeness in marriage as we go from being relative "strangers" to becoming "family"?

Here's a hint: We often treat strangers better than family.

Picture concentric circles. (For those of you who, like me, were a little bit allergic to math as kids, concentric circles are simply circles of ever-increasing size moving out from a point at the center—so if you wanted to draw concentric circles you'd draw a dot, then you'd make a small circle around it, then another, slightly bigger circle around that, etc.)

Now, as we bring people in, closer to the center from the outer circles, they become less like strangers and more like "family".

The problem is that as people become more like family to each other, their reactions and behaviors towards each other also become more like their reactions and behaviors from back when they lived with their families of origin, i.e. siblings, mom, dad, etc.

So as we become more and more comfortable with one another, our behavior changes as well, and usually not in a good way, but, instead, in less healthy, more childlike ways.

For most of us, these old reactions and behaviors of childhood and young adulthood are a FAR CRY from the Emotionally Competent, true adults we are trying to become in our current lives with the families we have now created, i.e. our spouses, kids, etc.

One of the major pitfalls of marriage and other long-term relationships is that, as we move in from the outer circles closer to the inner-most ones, we are moving into what I call the "Emotional Boiler Room".

Once we've placed someone in our Emotional Boiler Room, our reactions and behaviors towards them tend to be less adult and more childlike, less polite and considered, more impulsive and raw. We become more reactive towards them. We comment MORE and listen LESS. (Remember LVAC?)

As we approach the inner circle—the Emotional Boiler Room—our ability to hold back our immediate responses and emotional reactions lessens, and our impulse to react in a knee-jerk fashion grows.

We lose those special bits of formality, politeness, and deliberateness in our behaviors, and, instead, they get the more childlike part of us, which is less likely to truly listen, less likely to have empathy and to think about them even when we don't want something in return from them (e.g. favors, sex, money); AND less likely to use a modicum of restraint with them.

In other words, they essentially get a child for a spouse instead of an adult.

Now, if I had a dollar for every couple I've known that has had problems with physical intimacy (sex) in their marriages, I'd be, well, I'd be a better philanthropist let's put it that way.

The fact is that if the way our spouses reference us in their conscious, pre-conscious, or subconscious minds is as "child", then we can FORGET about either emotional OR physical intimacy with them.

In the end, the point is that we really DON'T want our spouses to become "family". Not like this anyway, where someone ends up playing the maladjusted child and the other the incompetent parent.

And we DON'T want to have them dwell in our Emotional Boiler Rooms either.

Instead, we want to keep that feeling and that respect that we had for them when we first met; that sense of awe and specialness, and also that sense of really liking them and wanting to be around them.

Now if you've read any of my other books—or the previous chapter in this one—you probably already know about the term Emotional Credibility. But, just in case you don't, Emotional Credibility = trusting the other person + liking them and wanting to be around them.

Now let me just say that, as a simple doctor, I certainly don't hold a corner on the market of the meaning of true love.

In fact, I confess that I'm not even sure what the word "love", as we commonly use it, means at all—except that over the past 20 years or so I've seen people profess their love for one another, only to then proceed to emotionally and spiritually torture and kill each other consistently and systematically over time.

The other thing about the word love is that, even after all these years of working with people, I still don't quite know what it would truly take for us humans to be able to profess our love for someone and to actually mean it and stand behind it not only with our words, but with our behaviors as well.

But I DO have an informed sense that, unless we are working on becoming true, Emotionally Competent Adults, we are not qualified, in my opinion, to use the word love the way we're always trying to use it, that's for sure!

However, Emotional Credibility—now THAT'S something we ordinary humans can work with!

If I am to build up Emotional Credibility with the people I profess to "love", then I must be actively working on accomplishing two things: 1) earning their trust (more below), and 2) making it easier for them to actually LIKE me and enjoy having me around.

On the old show "The Honeymooners", someone once asked Art Carney's character how he liked his job with the city, working down in the sewer system.

His response? (paraphrased) "Oh, it's a living and it don't bother me too much."

The way our spouses would respond—if they were being brutally honest!—to how they liked being married to us could probably run quite a gamut, but let me tell you that a LOT of what their answers would depend upon is the degree of Emotional Credibility we have with them:

A lot of Emotional Credibility (or what I call "E.C. Points ") would equal "Awesome!"

Mediocre E.C. Points = see Art's answer above..

Very little or minus E.C. Points = "Horrible"..."I basically hate being around him/her and I try to avoid him/her whenever possible. I'd rather be alone."

But please know that, as we and our spouses go from that outer-circle towards that inner-circle or Boiler Room, we don't always have to slide into that childhood, reactionary, impulsive, disrespectful, inconsiderate, non-Deliberate, knee-jerk, defensive, 'comfortable', family of origin position with them.

By using the concept of Emotional Credibility, which tells us to build trust by using the LVAC model (Listen, Validate, Ask, Comment), as well as other adult skills such as restraint, we have begun to construct a map and a method by which we can actually—perhaps one day—say the words "I love you" to our spouses and have it mean something real in our adult lives.

CHAPTER 16

ADULT NEUTRALITY (Y)

What do you think about when you think of the word 'neutral'?

Do you think about Switzerland?

Do you think about not taking sides, or about not caring either way about a particular issue?

Well, I have a completely different definition of Adult Neutral for you, a behavioral one that has to do with what I call true Adult Emotional Competence.

When we are behaving in an adult neutral way, we are behaving in an 'emotionally clean' way.

In other words, we are not reacting based upon our past hurts and subconscious agendas.

Adult emotional neutrality is a deliberate mode, not a reactive mode. We are 'clean' of our childlike states of mind and habits, where there is usually someone to blame or where we are somehow powerless, agitated victims who are enraged, rejected, abandoned, or betrayed.

Though this victimhood very likely really did happen to us in childhood, it is often not really happening to us the same way in adulthood. However, the feelings most definitely can be the same today as they were back then, just as though they had been saved in one of those zip-lock baggies.

The problem though, is that we are often behaving and reacting based upon these old wounds and feelings without even knowing it, and we are often hurting the people around us in our current lives today with these reactions to the past.

So, for example, when I am behaving in an adult neutral way with my spouse, I am NOT in a reactive mode with her, meaning letting all of my childlike impulses and conflicts rule my behaviors with her. Instead, I am behaving in an emotionally clean way, without all of the emotional noise of the past controlling me.

Example:

"Honey, there's been a change in schedule and I need to take the kids to an extra rehearsal tonight, so we'll have to postpone dinner until later."

Non-Adult Neutral Response: "Oh, you have GOT to be kidding me! Again! This is always happening now, ever since they got that new music teacher...."

More Adult Neutral Response: "Wow, ...okay, so we'll have to figure out how this will work. Call me later, honey."

Notice how, in the first response, I went with my knee-jerk, reactive, childlike response to a particular turn of events in life, something which happens all the time. There is really nobody to blame, but I blamed and became angry anyway. I created a maelstrom, a tornado even. Batten down the hatches, here comes the angry victim child!!!

Not very adult-like. And definitely not emotionally clean of all of my childlike behaviors and reactions. The past has ruled the day again, and my present, true adult self is buried somewhere deep beneath it.

And now my wife has another child to deal with.

Not good for the trust or the intimacy between us. Yet it happens to couples all the time.

My friends, we behave in non-adult neutral ways ALL-THE-TIME.

At home.

At work.

At the store.

With our neighbors and friends.

With our kids.

This last one is particularly damaging, because we lose our professional role as parents when we treat our children in non-adult neutral ways; we become their peers instead of their parents.

Example:

"Dad, can you help me fix this?"

Non-Adult Neutral Response: "What!? Again? What did you do!? I'll help you, but this is the last time!" (Like a child throwing a hissy fit—might as well have been a non-cooperative, selfish, not-so-nice friend instead of the child's parent. And that, by the way, is exactly the amount of respect and trust that will be earned by the parent in this example.)

More Adult-Neutral: "Fine, but you'll have to give me a couple of minutes, I'm in the middle of something."

In the first response, the father is clearly upset at being interrupted and pulled away from whatever he was doing. His childlike, reactive self feels put-out, cheated, and perhaps even threatened and betrayed by his child's request. Maybe subconsciously he's still a child who is fighting to not be controlled or intruded upon by his mother or father.

Plenty of noise there from the past. Not clean. Not adult-neutral.

But, of course, he doesn't actually consciously know any of this—he just reacts to it, acts it out.

Although these examples may seem a bit obvious and extreme compared to your particular situation, they do illustrate what we 'adults' do all the time.

That is, we may LOOK like adults and we may do our jobs like adults, but, often, in the way we comport ourselves with others—especially with our loved ones—we do not BEHAVE like neutralized adults; we are, instead, still ruled by the past.

True, adult, emotionally competent behavior is Adult Neutral behavior. It is clean of the voices and hurts of the past which have embedded themselves deeply into our subconscious minds and therefore into our behaviors and reactions. Whether it was our parents' reactivity towards us as children or other early influences and traumas, you can bet that these voices and hurts of the past are here—in the present—big time within us!

You can also bet that they will have continued rule over us, and on our current behaviors, unless we consistently and tirelessly work to neutralize them.

It's okay to fail; just don't ever give up.

CHAPTER 17

HOW TO REVERSE TIME (K)

In every family, if you go back far enough through the generations, there is some form of tragedy.

Maybe it was the destruction and losses of war. Or perhaps there was a complete loss of fortune or property. Or maybe there were drugs and alcohol or violent acts. Perhaps it was murder or rape or other horrible examples of man's inhumanity towards his fellow man; or maybe something entirely different occurred, like a parent, grandparent, or great-grandparent stricken with severe mental (or physical) illness.

Whatever the case may have been, the result was that the generations afterward felt the effects of these traumas whether directly and in obvious ways, or indirectly in more subtle ways.

You see, we humans, whether we are aware of it or not, are absolutely affected by the traumas of the generations before us even if sometimes in very subtle ways, and we pass the effects of these traumas down the generations via our various behaviors and personality traits which were originally meant only for sheer survival.

So even if we ourselves or our parents didn't suffer through one of the great calamities I've listed above, we do suffer what I call the "shell of the trauma" as it gets passed down to us, then to our children, etc., through the CHANGES in personality of the original survivor.

Think about it for a moment: if you yourself survived one of the traumas above, then it would make sense that, even though you survived it, you did CHANGE because of it as well.

Trauma requires that—in order to survive it—we CHANGE. Thus the term "survivor."

We humans "survive" trauma, but it leaves its indelible mark on us; on our hearts, on our minds, and on our souls.

Let's say that great granddad survived World War I (or II depending on your age), but he came home with all the signs of what we would now call PTSD (Post Traumatic Stress Disorder)—quick temper, poor impulse control and a sense that life could end at any minute, mood swings, problems sleeping, etc.

Granddad then gets married and has children. Guess what? With these CHANGES embedded within his personality, he now has to deal with his wife, his children, and with his post-trauma life itself. It doesn't take a rocket scientist to figure out that his family will very likely be on the receiving end of these CHANGES.

So what does that potentially mean?

It means the kids will get yelled at quicker, he'll lose it faster, he'll be overwhelmed more easily and act more erratically; maybe he'll use alcohol or gamble or have affairs to escape his pain. Whatever it is, these CHANGES in him, though he supposedly "survived" his trauma, are transmitted to his children by his very reactions and interactions with them. By his very personality and the CHANGES embedded deeply within it.

Now they've been traumatized too from exposure to him. And guess what again? They will pass the "shell of the trauma" from their interactions with their CHANGED father down to their own children—even though they themselves were never in the war, and nor were their children, they have most certainly been exposed to it by proxy, intergenerationally, via the shell of the original trauma that their father experienced.

So the kids of the kids of the traumatized man are now traumatized too. They have been hurt by the "shell of the trauma"—i.e. the very CHANGES in granddad which resulted from his original traumas and which may have even helped him survive the original trauma in the first place. Traits like quick impulses to react and a degree of hypervigilance may have helped granddad survive on the battlefield, but now, with his family, these personality CHANGES can cause fear and anxiety in his loved ones and traumatize THEM too.

And it's the same with all of our own adaptive CHANGES that come from our own particular traumas—we pass them along to our children and they to theirs, over and over again as the "shell of the trauma" which we were originally exposed to. It's in our personalities—our reactions, our fears, our hypervigilance and anxiety, our impulsiveness, our defensiveness and our sensitivities.

In every case, our very personalities have CHANGED and have been shaped either directly by original traumas, or by parents who have passed on the "shell of the trauma" down to us via their own personality adaptations to their original traumas OR the "shells" that were passed down to them.

The thing to realize is this: What were once useful and perhaps critical CHANGES for survival become destructive and self sabotaging personality traits and unhealthy "defense mechanisms." They get in the way of true emotional intimacy and connectedness with our loved ones and within ourselves, and they perpetuate the original traumas forward through future generations.

The way we can "reverse time" and help neutralize our traumas is by using the LVAC Technique.

It is really very simple: When we do LVAC with someone (which stands for Listen, Validate, Ask, Comment), we are Commenting last, if at all. Notice how uncommon it is for people to communicate this way.

And a little secret I'll share with you is this: We pass our traumas onto the next generation with our Comments. These can either be Comments literally with our words, OR with our behaviors.

With LVAC, we are Listening first, then Validating what the other person (your child, for example) is saying. Then we Ask open ended questions to them about what they're saying so they can explore this with us and, thus, within themselves. This way we are giving them a chance to find out what THEY are thinking and feeling, rather than passing on OUR reactions and baggage to them, which we already know have been distorted and CHANGED by our parents' Comments to us.

Instead, we Comment last, if at all. This way, when we finally do make a Comment, in the form of an opinion or other such thing, it will at least be more accurate with regards to what's really going on with the person in front of you and less about the reactions ("shell of the trauma") that have been passed down to you.

Notice that the beauty of this method is that it forces us to Comment last.

It makes sense if you think about it: Our Comments come from OUR reactions, OUR opinions, OUR experiences, OUR filters in life, and OUR defense mechanisms. In other words, they come from OUR traumas, either direct ones, or indirect ones.

If we've already established that our original traumas or the "shells" which have been passed down to us CHANGE all of the things I've just listed in the previous paragraph, then it follows that we really can't trust our Comments to be very "neutralized" and emotionally "clean". In fact, they're loaded—loaded with our own traumas as well as those that were passed down to us by previous generations over time.

In your life you've probably noticed that if you want to learn about somebody the best thing you can do is listen. On the other hand, if you want others to learn about you, speak.

The trick, then, in "reversing time" is to not allow our raw, reactive Comments (words or behaviors) to come out on a daily basis, for this is the primary way that we transmit our traumas to our children, and, eventually, they to theirs. Instead, follow LVAC and you'll stop the trauma cycle in your family. And THAT, my friends, is like reversing time, along with the intergenerational transmission of the traumas that go with it.

CHAPTER 18

COMING IN FOR A LANDING: TIME AND MONEY IN YOUR MARRIAGE (M)

When we marry, there are two very important things which we no longer independently control in our lives, namely: time and money.

Our married lives are quite different from our single lives in many ways, and our attitudes about time and money are a huge part of that difference.

I call this change from single life to married life "coming in for a landing":

Single Guy: "I'm going out with the guys after work today for happy hour."

Married Guy: "Honey, the guys are thinking about going out on Thursday for happy hour. What do you think?"

Notice the differences. Single Guy is able to, quite on the fly, let people know what his plan already IS.

Married Guy, on the other hand, ASKS about his wife's thoughts regarding his plan, AND he gives her a few days' notice for when it's supposed to happen.

The reason for the differences in the above scenarios is based on that idea from Chapter 14 called Emotional Credibility.

Remember, Emotional Credibility equals trust + liking the other person and wanting to be around them.

When we continue to make independent decisions about time and money without communicating or processing first with our spouse, as though we were still single, we lose Emotional Credibility with them; and this is also an indicator that we have not yet come in for a landing from our single lives into our married lives.

Thinking about buying a new car? Better check in with your spouse and see if that'll be an appropriate family purchase at this time.

Thinking about moving? Better check in with your spouse and learn about his/her opinion regarding the financial aspects of that, as well as their own vision for your future domicile together.

Want to volunteer at a local shelter? Great idea! BUT, better see what your spouse is thinking too. (Charity—as well as proper communication—should start at home.)

You see, once we marry, we have, in effect, agreed to a few things:

First, we've agreed to be accountable to the other person.

Second, we've agreed to be more deliberate and responsible about our behaviors and decisions.

And third, we've agreed to be honorable with regards to our spouse's feelings and opinions, and with the trust they've placed in us.

(Of course, we've also agreed to other things as well, including fidelity, empathy, compassion, support, and encouragement, among others.)

If we follow through on these things we build the trust and our spouses like us more and want us around more of the time (i.e.

Emotional Credibility increases). If we do not, they can feel betrayed by us and resentful towards us and we lose Emotional Credibility with them.

Work with your spouse on communicating what you want, don't want, like, and don't like, as well as what you feel you need or don't need. You are no longer a free agent; you've signed onto a team now.

Never assume that they'll just "know" or that they should just "know" or "agree". They don't and won't, and they'll resent you for thinking that they did or should have.

Make it a lifelong goal for your lives together to get to know each other every day by Listening, Validating, Asking open ended questions, and saving your Comments (either in word or behavior) for last. (The LVAC technique was discussed in the previous chapter, as well as back in Chapter 6.)

So remember, when it comes to time and money, marriage requires that we be accountable, honorable, and deliberate with these valuable, limited resources in order to preserve the Emotional Credibility and the healthy emotional connection between spouses.

CHAPTER 19

ARE THE HOLIDAYS 'HAPPY' FOR YOU? (Y)

I'm often told by folks how difficult various holiday seasons are for them throughout the year, especially, for many of them, the big winter holiday season.

Sometimes it's losses we've suffered and the people who won't be with us anymore.

Sometimes it's bad childhood experiences which are amplified evermore by the general emotionality and intensity of the season.

And sometimes it's simply the great buildup and stress of expectations, energy expenditures (and other expenditures), family reunions and celebrations, and earnest hopes for joy and for lasting changes for the new year.

It's this third scenario that I'd like to take a look at in this chapter.

How good are you at defining and handling your expectations of special occasions?

What DO you expect for the next holiday season? Have you, in a deliberate way, given yourself just a few minutes to ask this question?

It seems so ironic that one of the first things that happens to us humans around the more intense, special times of our lives—such as the holidays—is that we disconnect from ourselves.

You know the way it goes:

You've waited so long for the Big Event, there's been so much buildup and so much fantasizing and worrying about how it will go, who you'll see or won't see, the impression you'll make, the things you'll talk about or do together—all of this and more.

THEN, by the time the actual day or days come, you're so riled up and disconnected that you don't even enjoy it.

This is often the most significant reason behind the "holiday blues" which so many people face each year; there's just no way that the reality can match the fantasy, and, therefore, disappointment abounds. That, plus the disconnect within ourselves by the time the holiday is actually here, all adds to the distress and the general uneasiness we feel.

What if, the next time you face a Big Event or holiday, you make a promise to yourself to remain present and to deliberately experience the people, places, and things that surround you?

What does this mean?

It means you don't have to control it.

It means that it doesn't have to be perfect.

It means that you don't have to constantly perform for or please everybody.

And it means that you don't have to expect anything.

How would this be different for you?

I'll never forget back when my wife and I planned our wedding (read: she planned, I nodded yes a lot).

One of the most memorable parts of the experience for me was hearing my wife declare that she planned to enjoy her wedding day.

Enjoy it?

Back then, as a budding psychiatrist and still in the midst of the hectic turmoil of medical school, the thought hadn't even crossed my mind.

But she was right: Some things are meant to be enjoyed, not just survived, or, worse yet ruined because of the perceived demands of the occasion that we put upon ourselves.

Can you imagine, next holiday season, letting yourself enjoy the ride?

If you are playing host during some of it, can you be true enough to yourself to not totally exhaust and disconnect from yourself while preparing?

When we are exhausted and disconnected, we not only seldom enjoy the event itself, but our behaviors towards others are also less intimate and true. After all, if I'm totally stressed out and over-tired, I really won't have anything left to actually connect with or feel connected to anyone, including myself.

And if I haven't the energy to connect, then I may miss an important chance to re-connect with some important people in my life, including me.

With some of that extra energy and connection with myself and with others, I may even be in a position to do what we hardly ever get to do in our day to day adult lives: forgive and express love.

When was the last time you told a sibling you loved them?

What about the last time you helped one of them (or someone else) understand that you forgive them, either in words or in deed?

Can you picture yourself giving them a big hug, maybe even a kiss (okay men, stop laughing), and telling them that you love them and wish them good health and happiness? Life is short, and, unfortunately, the generations come and go by so quickly. As the old Italian saying goes, one that I heard many times while growing up: "They grow up and we grow old."

So many of our disconnects, both within ourselves, and within our families, begin with neglect of these relationships in addition to any actual affronts which may have occurred. This means that when we do not tend to these relationships, eventually bad feelings can seep into them even when nothing in particular is wrong, leaving us feeling disconnected and estranged.

So for the next holiday season, let me help you start the ball rolling by wishing you a loving, warm, healing, and connected holiday season!

CHAPTER 20

BECOMING AN 'ACTIVE LISTENER' (Y)

Are you an 'active listener'?

When most of us think about listening, we think of it merely as a pause between opportunities to speak.

Instead of relegating listening to a secondary place amongst our communication skills, what if we were to try to hone and perfect 'active listening' as a PRIMARY communication skill?

What is 'active listening'?

Active listening is listening with a PURPOSE.

It is ENGAGED listening.

When we listen actively, whether it be to our kids, our spouses, our coworkers, or our friends and neighbors, we are listening with not just our ears, but with our hearts, our minds, and our spirits; we are listening with empathy, with creativity, with our imaginations and with our fantasies, and we are listening with the INTENTION of understanding the other person as best we can.

When we Listen like this, we are truly trying to connect and to create emotional intimacy with others.

The human spirit craves this sort of connectivity and, unlike intimacy of the physical variety, it really can and should be had with as many other people as possible in order to give us a sense of belonging and feeling settled inside and in our lives. (Of course, when we work on Listening and creating emotional intimacy in our marriages, it elevates that relationship—both emotionally AND physically—beyond what it otherwise would be and it helps each spouse heal like never before.)

Also, when we Listen as described above, we can naturally leverage that Listening into an even greater understanding of the other person and where they're coming from by doing the rest of my LVAC technique with them as well; namely, Listening, Validating, Asking open-ended questions, and saving our Comments for last.

But the main point I want to convey is that listening is NOT a secondary activity behind speaking.

In order for us to become active listeners, we must learn to Stop and to realize that Listening is as much an adult skill as anything else and it must be deliberately cultivated, practiced, and honed with our energy and our intention.

Listening IS the main event, along with our empathy for the other person's position (Validation), and our Asking them questions to help clarify what they are trying to say. With children this is particularly powerful, but so to with adults.

I've often wondered what would happen to us if we lost the ability to speak except for asking questions.

In fact, I wrote a short story about this called "The Father" which you can read on my website www.LVACNation.com (just look under Bonus Features—I've formatted it so you can read it on the go with your cell phone.)

In the story, a disabled father raises his children successfully even though he can barely speak without losing his breath and even though he is quite physically limited. When I wrote this story I was trying to answer the question, "What is the absolute, bare-bones essence of what we're supposed to be giving to our children?" I wondered if it had to do with our conversations with them, our participation in sports and other activities with them, time spent together, our values, or what?

I found that, ultimately, and where it counts the most, Listening was the answer. If this intrigues you as much as it did me, I think you'll like the story.

In the end, it's up to us to find the presence of mind and the personal tranquility required to be able to become active listeners.

But please know the following: Becoming an active listener will require a 'gear shift' internally, as you come to face your need to be all 'revved up' inside: ready to speak, defend, comment, etc.—and, instead, as you shift towards allowing yourself to calm down, wait a moment or two, and really Listen with energy and intention.

I guarantee you that you will grow with this, and that you will earn greater Emotional Credibility (trust + likability) with others.

CHAPTER 21

Man–Boys and Angry Wives (M)

Ladies, we men may start out as what I call "man-boys", but we are trainable if you give us a chance.

It is in my first marriage book, entitled, Don't Get Married! (Unless You Understand A Few Things First), that you'll find the original man-boys and angry wives chapter.

In that chapter, I wrote:

"In a marriage [or marital-type relationship], many men initially have a difficult time making the transition to fully accepting the fact that, as of the day of their weddings, they have agreed to a larger agenda and goal now: to continuously work on building and customizing a life with their wives."

The problem is that many of us never fully realize the above consciously, so we half-innocently go about our lives as though nothing's really changed since the day of the wedding.

It's only half-innocent though, because although it may be that nobody's ever helped clue us in or helped teach us the right way, we're not children anymore either, so we ARE ultimately responsible for our choices and our behaviors now.

But, meanwhile, this lack of understanding causes problems, and it's how we help create the Angry Wife part of the dynamic:

"Angry wives are in large part created as a result of these major disappointments or "shocks", combined with whatever they themselves (the wives) bring into their marriages from past hurts and disappointments perhaps not immediately related to their husbands but triggered by them today."

So there we have it: a recipe for marital DISASTER.

As time goes by, the man continues to try to live his life the way he knows how, and the wife continues to build up resentment and mistrust in her man as she experiences disappointment after disappointment and hurt after hurt.

Needless to say, the sex, or physical intimacy, eventually goes out the window as well, along with the emotional intimacy and trust—and THIS is what often finally gets the man's attention.

Next, I'm going to give you three examples of 'man-boy' types, which are based on the ones I've written about before:

1) The sportsman type

2) The social animal type

3) The no-job-no-ambition type

(By the way, none of these are 'put downs' or judgments on any man—they're just an attempt at a common language that we can use, made by a recovering man-boy, in order to help you recognize and describe one of his own.)

Let's start with the sportsman type. And, again, let's begin with what I've written before:

"This is the man-boy whose angry wife is resentful because of all the time he spends playing in after work sports leagues, playing fantasy football, or playing cards, gambling, or otherwise focusing on regularly planned activities which do not involve her at all."

The problem here is that, once we marry, the meaning of time changes:

"To an overwhelmed, harried, busy wife, especially if there are kids involved or a career, even a few hours once or twice a week in which her husband is engaging in some sort of activity independent of her and the project of their lives together can present a conflict. He is spending this extra time away from not only her, but from the life they are trying to build together, which should be his first priority."

Next, the social animal type:

"This one seems to engender even more anger and resentment from the wives, than the first kind. This is the guy who tries to continue to hang out with his (usually unmarried) buddies from college, professional school, or work. It could be happy hour on Wednesday nights or meeting up with them on the weekends, all while his wife is either working, taking care of the kids, or managing the household."

And, finally, the no-job-no-ambition type, which might sound a bit harsh, but is meant with no disrespect—in fact, just the opposite:

"Unless you are physically or mentally disabled, which I'm assuming you and your wife would know about, you are pretty much obligated to engage in some sort of productive work activity in your life. Above all, the perception by your wife that you are either lazy or incompetent will breed anger, resentment, and, eventually contempt."

Now that we've looked at these three descriptions, let's look at that "trainability" part I mentioned earlier.

Men are unique and different from women in several important ways, two of which are as follows (incidentally, these are both generalizations since they may not be universally true for every man, woman, or couple):

1) Men are wired to feel more emotionally intimate when they are having, are about to have, or have had PHYSICAL intimacy (i.e. sex), whereas women are generally wired to feel more sexually available when they are feeling more EMOTIONALLY intimate with us. So men and women are, as you can see, wired quite differently from one another in this way, generally speaking.

2) Men have what I call a built in boyhood "kamikaze" reaction. In the past I have described it as follows: "One thing I've observed about men is that, once they sense that they are already seen as failures or as having failed in their spouses' eyes, they almost all tend to become angry in return, as they conclude that they've irreversibly messed up." (From my book, Don't Get Married! Unless You Understand a Few Things First.)

What happens in the kamikaze reaction is the old, "I screwed up and now she's mad/disappointed already, so forget it (or other 'f' word) all!"

So, if you know these two things, you also know that:

1) You and he need to rebuild the Emotional Credibility (which equals trust + liking each other) before there can ever be healthy emotional OR physical intimacy—in other words, you have to work together to help him go from man–boy to man so you can trust, respect, and like him again.

and

2) Quoting myself from the aforementioned marriage book: "Women who are becoming angry and resentful towards their husbands will get much more mileage (and results!) by first trying to gently support the husbands' efforts to change instead of immediately going on the attack."—So, in other words, try not to immediately punish him or withdraw from him (i.e. get 'cold'), which will only trigger the boyhood "kamikaze" reaction in him.

Well, there it is in VERY BRIEF summary.

In closing this chapter, my final, parting words to you men are as follows: Don't feel too badly about what I've just explained. It's just a matter of building up your skills, and that's exactly all that they are: skills. You are more than capable of improving them.

And to the women: Seek to understand the realities of the man-boy in your life and you'll have an easier time dealing with him and helping him along as he grows into the man you need him to be.

Now, as I always say: Get out there and help each other grow up!

CHAPTER 22

CONTENTMENT VS. AMBITION: WHY NOT BOTH? (Y)

Someone once asked me if I thought they should have more contentment in their life or more ambition.

Contentment VERSUS ambition? Why the false dichotomy?

I mean, really. Why must we choose to be *either* contented *or* ambitious?

I suppose the idea is that if we are truly contented, then we would not need to be quite so ambitious; ambition in this case carrying the connotation of not being satisfied or happy with one's life.

But what if we looked at it differently?

What if we looked at new connotations to the two words contentment and ambition?

For example, we could have contentment trigger thoughts of having a foundation; of feeling settled and committed to the set of basic choices one has made in one's life such as choice of spouse, having or not having children, living and participating in one's community, one's choice of profession, one's religious or spiritual beliefs, etc.

And perhaps ambition might call forth a feeling of activation of the self; of passion and of evolution. Ambition can be 'sexy'; it can add a certain mojo to our adults lives, including to the things that we've committed.

So, first of all, in going along with all of this, let's say that you're a married person with children, a house, a job or career of some sort, a couple of hobbies or avocations, and some friends.

Secondly, let's also say that you've still got dreams of what you'd like to be in the world or how you'd like to express your true self to the world through what makes you uniquely you.

Given these two assumptions, I think that a very high quality way to live—and one that I would recommend highly—would involve taking both of these elements and MAXIMIZING them together.

What does this mean?

It means maximizing our commitments to the things we've deliberately chosen to include in our lives, (e.g. spouse, children, job, friends, etc.), AND also maximizing our attempts to express our truest selves within the lives that we've chosen to have.

So, for example, you might be a husband and dad who's an accountant by day, but a volunteer firefighting hero by night.

Or maybe you're a wife and mom who runs the household-and-kid-company by day, but a rock star karaoke singer, local theater performer, or entrepreneur by night.

Or maybe you're a salesperson and a spouse by day, but a hotshot green-thumb organic gardener on the weekend.

My point here is that, in order to live our fullest lives we need to be able to do two seemingly disparate things at the same time: be committed AND be passionate—take our vows seriously AND make some new ones that continue to provide new challenges.

I'm often asked why it is that people act out by having affairs, or by using drugs and alcohol, or why it is that people leave their kids and spouses to 'start new lives'. Or, more recently, what the big thrill is to all the 'sexting' that's apparently going on, from married Federal government officials on down to local civil servants.

I think that part of the reason why people act out in these ways is that they haven't yet got the above balance down; i.e. they haven't yet mastered the skill of having Commitment PLUS Passion—Contentment AND Ambition.

So let's not fool ourselves.

We cannot live happy, fulfilling, and joyous lives with minimal guilt or regrets if we are not, first of all, committed to our lives.

BUT we also need to regularly challenge ourselves by exploring our hearts and by listening to what's in there.

The result will be a life with both a track record of following through with our promises and choices, as well as one in which we've continuously evolved both within and around those commitments. Commitment PLUS Passion. Contentment AND Ambition.

The alternative is a life story filled with broken promises, half-filled dreams, and abandoned casualties strewn about everywhere—with regret full steam ahead.

Chapter 23

Building Emotional Credibility With Your Teen (K)

Parents often tell me that their teens are driving them crazy.

A common theme is that the teen thinks that the parent is stupid and that they don't (ever) know what they are talking about. Needless to say, another commonality is that the teen "just doesn't listen to me."

Well, if you've read some of the previous chapters in this book already, you're familiar with the term Emotional Credibility.

Emotional Credibility consists of two simple things: trust and likability. When we can trust somebody enough to talk to them about difficult things, we naturally begin to like having them around more.

The problem is that many parents have long ago lost Emotional Credibility (E.C. for short) with their children, who then eventually become those seemingly monstrous teens and 'tweens.

And by the time this happens, the kid is older—and in some cases, quite a bit larger—and can do more damage to themselves and to others, in addition to cars, the house, etc.

When and how did the E.C. get lost?

To answer this, we must first take a brief trip back to when the child was really little.

Remember the terrible twos?

Well, we might as well think of them as a preview of the pre-teen and teen years, only the child is smaller and less potentially destructive.

The basic underlying principle is the same for both the toddler and the 'tween/teen: The child is testing limits and trying to get to know themselves and their surroundings better (including us), which is messy.

It's important to know that the way we reacted (or overreacted) to that little child when they tried to test these limits by doing crazy things (like putting oatmeal in the VCR—wait, there are no VCRs anymore—I'm getting old!), helped determine their future image of us and how we handle ourselves and our lives.

So, for example, if little Billy tried to feed himself but made a big mess and you flipped out or tried to prevent him from feeding himself entirely to prevent the mess, then little Billy's trust in you took a hit. And so did your general likability in his eyes.

You see, little ones don't have work or finances to focus on; they don't have kids of their own (usually) or houses or cars. So they focus on YOU.

They watch you and observe your behavior. In fact, they're pretty obsessed with observing you and learning what you can and can't handle (translation— what they can and can't do or say around you.)

In other words, they learn what kind of person you are.

Are you reasonably even-tempered, considerate, and slow to anger, reject, punish, shame, or withdraw your love?

Do you Listen, Validate, Ask (open ended) questions, then Comment last (i.e. the LVAC Technique from previous chapters)?

Or do you do the opposite? Comment first with some sort of judgment, immediate opinion, declaration, warning, or other some such projection of your anxiety agendas onto the child?

Well, dear reader, if I didn't do these things myself as a parent, I wouldn't know so well how to describe them to you.

The Emotional Credibility we earn with them in the earlier years will influence how rough their 'tween and teen years are on us.

Now here's the good news.

Even if you, like me, had your challenges in trying to keep calm and in restraining yourself and using the LVAC Technique when they were younger, now's your chance to start building up those E.C. points!

Do this: When your 'tween/teen criticizes you, try to not get defensive right away or feel immediately threatened somehow. Remember, you are—and always will be—their parent and they need you. You're the boss, so you have to act like it.

Picture yourself as a mountain and them as a smaller mountain that's trying to grow.

They can't actually move you or displace you.

Use my LVAC Technique (Listen, Validate, Ask, Comment) to build E.C. and to become a key person in their lives—someone they can come to and talk about anything with without fear of immediate comments, comparisons, judgments, knee-jerk "solutions", etc.

Try to remember that, more often than not, what they need from you is a stable, steady mountain that Listens to them.

Next, know that you must Validate their feelings and where they're coming from, and, along with that, perhaps Ask some open-ended questions. Save the Comments for last since they represent YOUR reactions and anxieties and they make the conversation about you instead of your child.

Don't make it about you. Let the child feel whatever they are feeling and let it be between them and the larger world around them; i.e. the things that they are trying to explore. Help them and guide them through the storm, but don't turn it around and make it about you by throwing yourself right in the middle of the chaos and fighting with them.

Picture a train coming straight for you: Then move out of the way. Guide, but don't try to control. Let it be about them learning about themselves in the world, not about them having to overcome the obstacle that is you.

If you want to rebuild and repair your Emotional Credibility with your 'tween or teen, you must: 1) realize when and how it was lost, and 2) use LVAC and your power of restraint as discussed in this chapter to build it back up.

Remember, keep it about them, not you, and everybody wins.

Chapter 24

Marital Expectations (M)

One of the most common mistakes in a marriage is to view each other as what I like to call "reference points for perfect mental health."

I can tell you this: If you think that your spouse is some sort of perfectly normal, put together person who should never or will never let you down or disappoint you, you can *fuggedaboutit!*

Your spouse is NOT a reference point for perfect mental health and neither are you (nor am I, and nor is my spouse, for that matter.)

We're all just somebody else's messed up kids, and we need to not forget that when dealing with and reacting to one another.

When we first meet our spouse, we do what's called "idealization".

In other words, we have a fantasy about who they are and what they're like and it's usually not all that accurate in real life, depending on the particular situation.

This fantasy, of course, comes tumbling down eventually, and then we're left with a whole lot of disappointment and resentment—and I've even heard "repulsion" and "disgust".

So, in summary thus far: At first our spouses are superstars who can do no wrong, then, eventually, they are giant disappointments who can do very little right.

This latter, eventual state of the relationship is what I call the "devalue phase".

The sad fact is that many marriages really never progress much further than these first two steps: idealize, then devalue. There's the initial idealization or "ga ga" phase, then, eventually, there are all the disappointments and resentments and maybe even some contempt thrown in for good measure.

In fact, in many marriages, the spouses never actually get to know each other for real at all—ever. Not the idealization phase, not the devalue phase, but reality. It doesn't get to ever happen.

It's not all that uncommon for a couple to have been married for twenty or more years and to tell me that, even after all that time, they really feel like they are strangers to one another.

Now let's get back to that idea I mentioned earlier about neither spouse being a reference point for perfect mental health.

It really comes down to this: We need to stop seeing our spouses as substitutes for the perfect, all giving, all caring parents we never had.

We must realize that our spouses are our peers, not our parents. We are supposed to give and take in a marriage, and we're supposed to work together and communicate through our problems. As I said before, we are each just somebody else's messed up kid after all.

So the next time your spouse doesn't do the right thing by you, try to tell them what you want in a respectful, compassionate, non-judgmental-but-non-apologetic way. Don't hold in your true feelings and build resentment towards them. And don't immediately act out with sarcasm or with belittling, shaming, or blaming tones.

Try to never assume that you really know each other or that you already know what the other person is thinking or feeling.

Instead, be prepared to get to know each other through a steady diet of Listening, Validating, Asking open-ended questions, and, if necessary, Commenting last (i.e. the LVAC Technique, as mentioned elsewhere in this book).

Remember, each person goes into their marriage as "just somebody else's messed up kid", and they're going to need to use the marriage to heal and to grow as individuals.

Another technique is to try and act the opposite of the way you would normally react with your spouse:

If your tendency is to hold it all in, start to trust more and share with them, even if you're angry or disappointed with them.

If your tendency is to let it all come out and to hold nothing back, start to learn to restrain a little since you might be overwhelming them perhaps like their caregivers did when they were children.

If you tend to get angry and snap back right away, practice restraint and let the strong pulse of anger pass—at least a little bit—before you speak.

If you tend to need to fix everything, step back a little and Listen more without trying to fix or conclude.

If you tend to be anxious and always in a rush, try to take it down a notch or two and give the people around you (and yourself!) a chance to find some tranquility for a few moments.

If you need to keep busy all the time, learn to Stop.

If you never say "I'm sorry" or "Thank you", start practicing saying these things.

If you need your spouse to quickly answer your questions or somehow make you feel better right away or fix the situation, try to back off a little bit and give yourself the opportunity to begin to learn to deal with your anxiety.

If you need to be in control of things all the time, ease up on that a little.

And—perhaps above all—deliberately invite your spouse to give you feedback about your behavior, even if it's not exactly going to be pleasant. You need to be able to trust each other with your observations of one another, as well as of your lives together.

So, in summary: Please remember that neither you, nor your spouse is a reference point for perfect mental health. You are each simply somebody else's messed up kid. So try to treat each other with more consideration, more compassion, and, in general, more gently. And, by all means, if you are having particular trouble with anger, anxiety, or anything else that makes it hard for you to reasonably control yourself with your spouse, please go ahead and get some professional individual counseling for it.

CHAPTER 25

DOES YOUR WORK HELP MAKE YOU A BETTER PERSON? (Y)

The other day I had some challenges on the business side of running my practice and it took me a few days to finally work through them.

When I finally did so, I not only felt relief, but I was also grateful.

I was grateful that my work, in one way or another, always seems to push me towards more and more personal growth as I grow professionally, negotiating various situations and challenges as they come up day to day.

These two things, professional and personal growth, are intertwined quite intimately, as are personal growth and interpersonal relationships.

In fact, in the past I've written about something called The Bicycle of Life, where I described the two wheels as the Work Wheel and the Love Wheel, representing professional and relationship growth, respectively.

The Bicycle of Life theory is this: as we try to grow (and grow up) in life, the Work and Love Wheels of the Bicycle of Life represent the major opportunities in adulthood to learn about ourselves and to get back to who we really are. Our work and our relationships bring us back to ourselves; the selves we lost through the traumas and tribulations of childhood—more on this in a minute.

So, the other day, not only was I glad for the immediate relief of having solved a problem, I was also thankful that I had learned yet another new piece to the puzzle that is me—this particular time through the challenges on the Work Wheel.

It was at that point that my old Bicycle of Life theory came back to me again.

In childhood, we don't always get the opportunity to learn all that much about ourselves, depending on how closely the adults around us were able to Validate our feelings and Ask us open-ended questions, versus becoming angry or dismissive with us.

Kids don't necessarily know how to negotiate difficult or complex situations, much less the thoughts and emotions that often go with them, so the adults around them are the ones who really need to help them work their way through these things. I recommend using the LVAC Technique found elsewhere in this book.

Now because these childhood opportunities for gaining self-knowledge and self-awareness were so limited for most of us, our work and our relationships (i.e. the Work Wheel and the Love Wheel of the Bicycle of Life), represent a sort of 'second chance' at finding or re-finding ourselves in adulthood.

The bottom line is this: You will learn a great deal about yourself through your work and your relationships. This includes how you respond to difficulties and conflict, changes, intimacy, your various impulses, and to commitments. It also includes how you communicate your thoughts and feelings in various situations and interactions with others.

So why bother with all this?

Because you stand to gain an invaluable degree of self-awareness and self-actualization if you look at your life as a series of events and situations which can teach you the intimate details of who you are through the Work and Love Wheels.

CHAPTER 26

LVAC FOR ASPERGER'S (K)

If you have a child or a spouse with Asperger's Syndrome, or if you yourself think that you may be an "Aspie", you may find this chapter interesting and useful.

One of the major challenges for adults and children with Asperger's Syndrome is the difficulty in accurately interpreting and modulating anxiety as well as dealing with the greater environment around them. These folks are often stuck in a vaguely defined distress- or pre-distress-fraught emotional space, trying to identify or make sense of what's happening around them or TO them at any given moment.

LVAC:

LVAC is a technique I invented to maximize empathetic communication. There is plenty to be read about LVAC in this book, but, in brief, it was designed to help guide us to meeting the other person where they are emotionally rather than where we think they are or should be; and the way we accomplish this with the LVAC approach is by Listening, Validating, Asking, and Commenting last.

I think that this skill translates very well to communicating with an Aspie, where empathy—or really trying to be accurate about your understanding of where they are emotionally—can be extremely challenging.

So besides briefly discussing the LVAC technique itself, I'm also going to share some observations I have made about how it can be adapted for use with a child or adult with Asperger's

Syndrome. (Note: I won't be going into any neurophysiology, neuropsychiatry, neurochemistry, or neuroimaging, as these topics are beyond the scope of this book. I am also going to stay away from neuroanatomical terminology as it is not necessary for what I want to share with you.)

So, again, LVAC stands for Listen, Validate, Ask, Comment.

The gist of it is to hold your Comments for last. These Comments might include: 1) immediate answers or "solutions" to what YOU perceive to be the problem, 2) telling the person what YOU would do, 3) making a judgmental or concluding statement, and 4) asking a closed-ended question where the answer is already in the question, e.g., "You're not wearing *that* are you?!"

Some Examples of the Uniqueness of the Aspie:

Okay, now I want to share with you what I've learned about a few differences in trying to use LVAC (Listen, Validate, Ask, and Comment) with those on the spectrum.

Number One: You are dealing with a human being who is fundamentally wired differently than most of us. Given any stimulus, (noise, color, voices, depth, human emoting), what may occupy YOUR central attention very likely is NOT the main focus for them, or, on the other hand, they might be 'hyper-focused' on it. So, for example, if you are focused on color, they may very well be focused on shape or height or sound. If you are focused on the calming nature of something, they may be tortured by the anxiety-provoking, hyper-intense nature of that very same thing.

Number Two: Their anxiety, worry, and fear triggers—and how they overcome them—may well be VERY different from what they are for you. A stimulus or situation which you yourself might be able to overcome quite easily or with the help of some soothing words or touch might be very difficult to negotiate for an Aspie. Worry can become obsessive and extremely threat-laden for someone with Asperger's, so that when you are trying to soothe them, you have to be cognizant of this heightened vigilance to a threat that you yourself may very well NOT be perceiving. For example, a television program in a doctor's office, a song on the radio, or a smell in the air like a woman's perfume might each trigger an anxiety, worry, or fear response deep in the emotional-modulation parts of the Aspie's brain which you may not perceive or understand at the time.

Number Three: And speaking of the above, what might calm a non-Aspie down may very well further agitate someone with Asperger's—e.g. saying "you're just going to feel a bit of pressure" prior to an injection at the doctor's office may trigger a whole cascade of vague, undefined, and dark worry about what this word 'pressure' is supposed to mean in the context of getting an injection, causing a higher threat response. Becoming angry, incredulous, or indignant with their reaction or noncompliance will further agitate them. The more you display how frustrated you are with them or how much you DON'T understand what's happening to them, the more torturously lost, abandoned, and desperate they will feel. Given how already tenuous is their hold on feeling connected to you or to their environment in the first place, it doesn't take much for an Aspie child (or adult) to escalate once they start falling into the abyss of further disconnect from you and from their environment.

LVAC for Aspies:

So then, you've probably gathered that doing LVAC with an Aspie will often require more creativity, more effort, more inductive and deductive thinking, and, most of all, more heart. Maybe it should be called The Ultimate LVAC!

Practicing the LVAC Technique with anyone is difficult enough, because it goes against our nature to Listen first, Validate next, then to Ask open-ended questions that give the person space to talk, and, finally, to save our Comments for last. Instead, we like to Comment FIRST by answering, solving, or judging right away. With an Aspie, doing LVAC is going to take everything you've got.

Listening with Your 'Aspie Ear':

You're going to need to Listen with both of your ears, plus your third ear, what I call your Aspie ear.

The Aspie ear doesn't just hear within the context you're used to hearing. It hears on a much, much broader scale.

When Listening to a person with Asperger's—and this includes observing them even if they're not actually communicating verbally at the time—you've got to think of AS MANY POSSIBILITIES AS YOU CAN about what they are actually saying with their words or their behaviors. It's kind of like when we physicians make what's called a 'differential diagnosis': We list out all the possibilities of what MIGHT be causing the patient's presenting symptoms.

Your Aspie ear doesn't just 'hear' what is literally being said. Its intention is to hear what the Aspie MAY actually be feeling or communicating.

You're going to Listen like you've never listened before. You're going to be Detective Columbo (from the old T.V. show) and your Aspie ear is your tool.

Sometimes you're going to hear a very concrete, direct question, thought, or feeling, and that's fine. But, at other times, what you're going to hear is actually what I call a 'derivative' of what's really going on. This means, for example, that you may be THINKING that you are hearing happiness or silence, but what you are really hearing is worry, increasing anxiety and disconnect, and a pending outburst.

Validation:

Validation is very closely related to—and very often produces—both a calming effect and soothing in a person.

For a person with Asperger's, this is especially important as it can prevent escalation of their anxiety, worry, or fear reactions. It can, however, be exceedingly difficult to validate, especially if you haven't used your Aspie ear to first identify what is really happening for your Aspie.

What can be validating to one person, can be quiet invalidating to another, depending upon how closely we've first Listened to them and to their heart.

For someone with Asperger's, a random, uninformed, hug, touch, or word, may very well cause greater distress.

Asking vs. Commenting:

In order to Listen and to Validate the best we can, we often need to Ask one or more open-ended questions in order to learn more about what the other person is going through at the moment.

This can be especially challenging to do with an Aspie, as they may not have a clue themselves as to what they're feeling or why—they may just be in distress.

This is why asking OPEN ENDED questions is the best approach, because it will hopefully encourage and entice the Aspie to talk more so you can Listen more with your Aspie ear.

Examples of open-ended questions are: "What's up?", "How are you doing?", "Can you tell me more?", and, "What are you thinking about?"

Notice how I've stayed away from asking "How are you feeling?" This is generally a very low yield question in general, and especially with someone on the spectrum. Instead, appealing to their thoughts rather than directly to their emotions tends to get the conversation moving along more smoothly and productively.

Lastly, try to stay away from too much assuming, random guessing, or direct Commenting with your Aspie, as this can be almost immediately toxic and anxiety provoking for them.

Instead, use the approach I've described, which can be used with anyone, not just those with Asperger's, but tweak it the way I've described and observe for yourself the difference in your interactions with your Aspie.

CHAPTER 27

MARRIAGE IS AN EMOTIONAL LABORATORY (M)

One of the major goals of being a married person is to grow as an INDIVIDUAL.

In my book, Don't Get Married! (Unless You Understand A Few Things First), I describe marriage as an Emotional Laboratory for individual growth.

An Emotional Laboratory—how romantic, right?

Glad you're with me so far.

If it were up to me, gone would be the terms "Soulmate", "True Love", "In Love", and the dreaded, "I Love You But I Am No Longer IN Love With You...."

Instead, briefly, the Emotional Laboratory idea states that your job as my spouse is to allow yourself to take emotional risks with me to further your own emotional growth, and that my job is to do the same with you.

This way we each grow as INDIVIDUALS in the Laboratory, while at the same time growing as a couple as well.

One of the biggest problems with the way marriage is done is that people believe that they are supposed to make each other whole, or somehow save each other from the pain of life.

The Emotional Laboratory says that marriage is supposed to be for the growth of each individual spouse, who, in turn, uses the other one to learn to take emotional risks that they've been trained—sometimes from as early as childhood—to NEVER take.

So, for example, if your tendency is to "ready, fire, aim", then the Emotional Laboratory says that you must practice talking to your spouse about your feelings first, before you get mad, give up, yell, or complain. AND they must do the same with you.

If your tendency is to keep difficult topics or emotions to yourself (in order to save your spouse the pain, or to prevent them from rejecting or shaming you, or from becoming angry with you), the Emotional Laboratory says to share them instead.

Some classic, albeit, particularly difficult examples of using marriage as an Emotional Laboratory would be when tempted to act out around issues like infidelity, spending money, or scheduling your time.

Before you do any of these things, you must first go to your spouse and tell them that you are in trouble and that you are tempted to act out in these ways. Your spouse, by the way, has to vow never to summarily reject or shame you, or become angry or belligerent with you when you share things which are difficult for you to share, otherwise the Emotional Laboratory will never work.

We need to have trust in each other's reactions to difficult material in order for the Emotional Laboratory to work and to work well.

The way it's supposed to work is that one spouse takes an emotional risk by sharing something they would normally NEVER share with anyone else, and the other spouse uses a technique like my LVAC and Listens, Validates, Asks open-ended questions, and Comments last, if at all.

Use your spouse as a safe haven for your deepest and most painful, as well as your most joyous "secrets".

Train one another to receive these gifts from each other as a way of helping each of you grow into the strong, emotionally competent adult individuals you were meant to be.

For most people, childhood and young adulthood influences what they allow themselves to say to other people or to even acknowledge within themselves.

The Emotional Laboratory of marriage is a perfect opportunity for spouses to use each other to help repair the trust, the self-confidence, and the self-acceptance that many of us lose somewhere during the process of "growing up." It is a chance to learn to share again, without fear or shame, and to also learn how to truly Listen to another human being and to Validate their experiences.

One of the key goals in our marriages, as well as when raising our children, is to build Emotional Credibility (which you may recall from earlier chapters equals trust + being liked by the other person enough for them to want us around them.)

Use your marriage as an Emotional Laboratory and you will achieve plenty of Emotional Credibility with one another.

So remember, save the Comments for last (LVAC!), but don't save the secrets from each other anymore!

CHAPTER 28

DON'T GO TO A HOT ROD SHOP FOR AN OIL CHANGE (Y)

I regularly get phone calls from people seeking a new psychiatrist, and, though I must often tell them that I do not have any openings, I do try to get the basics of what they are looking for so that I might guide them to the next doctor or practice to call.

One of the distinguishing characteristics of these calls is that the person on the other end of the line has often already been—or is wondering if they need to be—labeled with a particular mental disorder.

Now, in some cases, as with the seriously and chronically mentally ill population, (e.g. disorders like schizophrenia and bipolar disorder), the person WILL eventually need to be diagnosed with a serious mental illness and treated with medications, sometimes heavy-duty ones with heavy duty long-term side effects.

However, I must say, as calmly as I can, that the practice of psychiatry has come to a point of near ridiculousness when it comes to over-diagnosing and over-medicating people way too soon in the process, and way too much in general. And this is, in my opinion, intimately related to the near disappearance of the well-rounded psychiatrist: one who does psychotherapy as well as psychopharmacology—but that is a whole other topic.

The great majority of people who contact my private practice looking for a new doctor are NOT chronically and seriously mentally ill.

However, too many of them have already been diagnosed and even treated for conditions like bipolar disorder or ADD. In fact, I couldn't begin to keep track of how many people have either diagnosed themselves or their loved ones with bipolar disorder just by watching a T.V. commercial about a drug used to treat this condition:

"Hi Doc, I think my husband is bipolar."

"No, your husband is probably a bit of a pain in the @ss, but he's not bipolar."

And if, per chance, the person calling happens to be a young person between the ages of 13 and 30, then there's a great possibility that they're going to somehow fit criteria for bipolar disorder in someone's eyes:

What other age group has soooo many "mood swings"?

What other age group is soooo impulsive or unpredictable?

What other age group is soooo risky in their behaviors?

What other age group is soooo likely to jump around from thought to though in their conversations?

Other new caller favorites are ADHD and Adult ADD:

"Hi Doc, I think my child has attention deficit."

"Yes, there IS an attention deficit, but we may need to look deeper at where exactly the deficit lies, including between the child and the adults around him/her."

Can't concentrate at your stressful job?

Thoughts seem to hop around in your head?

Are you easily distracted, especially when stressed?

Do you feel "wired" and fidgety on the inside?

Lacking follow-through? Impulsive?

"Of course!", you say, "I have all of the above so I must have ADD!"

The Problem With All This

The problem with all of this over-diagnosing and over-medicating too soon and too much is threefold:

1) It can be dangerous:

The newest marketing techniques involve direct-to-consumer T.V. commercials. Patients then take that information and bring it in to their primary care doc or psychiatrist and the rest is history.

They don't necessarily know, for example, that some of these medications were originally designed for schizophrenia or bipolar disorder and are now "FDA approved" (don't get me started on THAT topic) for conditions like major depression as well. But the problem is that other drugs are also available for major depression which do not carry as high a side effect profile as what they might have just seen advertised on T.V.—side effects like high cholesterol, high blood sugar, and heavy weight gain.

Just keep this in mind: Heavier meds originally designed for more serious conditions often carry heavier side effect burdens even if "only" being used for moderate depression. Of course, in cases of very severe depression, we can and should augment with some of these medications, but, importantly, not as an everyday first line option as the commercials would have you believe.

2) It can distract us from the underlying problems, wasting years of someone's lifetime:

If you're 18 and someone tells you that you "have bipolar" and starts you on a mood stabilizer or antipsychotic medication (or several of them), you may be in for years' worth of chasing different pills and pill-manager type M.D.s in order to get the "right" combination of psych meds.

At the same time, you may be allowed to be left totally ignorant of the fact that there are underlying themes which need to be processed in good talk-therapy work that can absolutely change your symptoms and brain chemistry over time.

But the option of customizing any medication use over time depending on what's happening in the talk-therapy work gets lost in the patient's "hope" of finally having a "diagnosis" and a "cure", which often includes the steps of diagnosis, medication treatment, and maintenance meds—without the talk-therapy part of the journey.

The focus becomes pills in cases where it should have been therapy work plus or minus pills, depending on what is getting done in the talk-therapy and how the person is changing over time.

On the other hand, this also points to the absolute importance of saving serious psychiatric diagnoses like bipolar disorder for the people that truly qualify for them, so that proper, often miraculous and life-saving medications can be started and maintained.

And, finally:

3) It can play on people's hopes of finally feeling better:

A lot of trust is placed on us doctors.

We take a Hippocratic Oath when we graduate from medical school in which we swear to practice medicine ethically and with the interest of the patient first.

People come to us in hopes of feeling better; with the belief that our training and our experience can help guide them towards relief of their pain.

But, as much as I hate to say it, medicine—and not just the specialty of psychiatric medicine—has become like any other business in which the old saying applies: Caveat Emptor, (buyer beware).

If you go to a doctor who only prescribes medications, you WILL get a medication. Which is why, especially with psychiatric issues, it's best to see an M.D. who is also a therapist as well.

I like to tell people that you need to find a psychiatrist with the heart of a psychologist or social worker.

In fact, if I were seeking psychiatric care, I'd ask prospective providers, "How do you feel about treating personality and circumstance-driven issues?", instead of stating, "I think I might have bipolar or ADD."

The former question will likely weed out providers who are primarily med-driven, whereas the latter will produce too many who are quite willing to medicate you quite early on in the process.

Again, and as I've qualified in each of the other two circumstances above, this does not hold for that minority of people who actually do, in fact, have a major psychiatric disorder such as severe, debilitating major depression, bipolar disorder, or schizophrenia.

But proper diagnosis, sometimes over time, is absolutely essential before putting pen to prescription pad.

Which brings me back to the title of this chapter:

Don't Go to a Hot Rod Shop for an Oil Change

If my car seems to need an oil change, or maybe a bit of maintenance or repair work, and I take it to a Hot Rod Shop, something quite interesting may very well happen.

That is, they may do a fine job on the oil change, if they remember to do it at all, but I will likely come out of there with a super-charged engine, extra fat tires, a sports transmission, modified exhaust, and racing stripes to boot—and I may still need to eventually get that oil change and core maintenance work done on my car at some point.

But who could blame them? For that's just what they do. And, after all, they aren't breaking any laws. In fact, they're probably very well respected in the community and have lots of experience.

So, in the end and in the face of all this, I would caution you and your loved ones to be careful about who's shop you walk into in the first place, especially if you're planning on the long term and not just a quick quarter-mile drag race.

Because, remember, if you seek a pill, a pill you shall always receive. But if you do your research, and seek a well-balanced approach, the road ahead may be longer and in some ways more difficult and devoid of "quick fixes", but the results will be more permanent—and more customized to the realities of who you really are and to your particular situation.

CHAPTER 29

LVAC STANCE (K)

If you already know about LVAC from my LVAC Nation! book, or from the Cobwebs and Ugly Wallpaper book, or from my blog, then I think you'll enjoy learning about the LVAC Stance which goes beyond simply memorizing and using the LVAC acronym.*
*(LVAC= Listen, Validate, Ask, Comment)

Now, we already know that by remembering to use the four simple LVAC steps in our daily communications with others, we are maximizing OUR understanding of what they are trying to say AND helping them to maximize THEIR self-understanding as well. And we know that by Commenting too soon, before Listening and Validating, we short-circuit both of these processes.

But we should also understand that there is a general Spirit of LVAC—an LVAC 'Stance' if you will—which basically says:

"Whenever someone is talking to me I'm going to try to relax, sit back, and observe. I'm going to make up my mind to take a position or stance of learning about what others around me are trying to say to me regarding how they are feeling or what they are thinking without interrupting them or waiting impatiently or anxiously for my turn. I'm not going to make it my chief priority to speak. My main goal is to Listen, not Comment. I will work on feeling centered and at peace with myself so that I can really be present when interacting with others, whether they be my kids, my spouse, or whoever else."

Make it a deliberate practice to approach your world with this stance. It is one of inquiry, of learning, and of truly connecting with others.

When you go through life constantly communicating your anxiety agendas by interrupting, one-upping, or otherwise Commenting right away with either words or behaviors, you lose the connection, as well as, eventually, the trust.

Do this often enough with your children or spouse and you will lose Emotional Credibility, which, you may recall from other parts of this book, consists of Trust + Likeability.

Now, go out there and practice your LVAC Stance!

Chapter 30

Saying 'I'm Sorry' (M)

How hard is it for you to say 'I'm sorry'?

If you think about it for a moment, you might imagine that in my line of work as a psychiatrist, I'm in the privileged position of being able to regularly witness and learn about interpersonal conflict.

I'd say that, on average in my professional life, I am either witness to or to some degree involved in, some sort of fairly intense interpersonal conflict from anywhere between six to twelve times per week, especially when couples are involved.

And one of the first things I learned, some years back, is just how truly difficult it is for people to utter the words 'I'm sorry' to each other.

'I'M SORRY.'

No, not, 'I'm sorry but...', or, 'I'm sorry if...'

Just, 'I'm sorry', period.

This ESPECIALLY holds true if the two people happen to be in a close relationship with one another, as is the case with married couples or between parents and their children.

I also noticed how hard it was for me as well.

What amazes me the most, however, is what I feel AFTER I give a proper, adult apology. To give justice to the feeling I would need to use words like 'cleansed', 'calm', 'loving', 'at peace', and, 'loved'.

In fact, when I listen to my devout religious friends talk about their experiences with God (as for me, I'm just a VERY imperfect Catholic who prays that God exists for fear of the alternative), they sometimes—incredibly enough—use words that look quite similar to my list above: loving, at peace, cleansed, and calm.

This can be some powerful stuff we're talking about here.

When we struggle to grow and to act as truly Emotionally Competent adults, we are, in a sense, praying to a higher, stronger, more capable and dependable power and self; one that we can TRUST and one that we can feel safe and good about sharing with our loved ones and the world around us.

This adult self is very different from the more childlike—but also powerful—habit and trauma driven REACTIVE self of our childhoods and earlier adulthoods.

When we apologize like true adults, we help both ourselves AND the other person feel better and heal from past betrayals. For many people—starting as far back as childhood for some—not a lot of people from their past really knew how to behave like Emotionally Competent adults in this way. Therefore, a proper adult apology to them now can help lay the groundwork for a new buildup of trust, which is VERY healing.

So what is a proper adult apology, then?

Consider this:

When I make an apology, say, to my wife or to my children, I am not simply saying 'I'm sorry'. I am applying the adult skill of Deliberately Stopping also.

THEN, I am checking in with myself and acknowledging what I am feeling. This would be like having my very own Emotionally Competent adult inside of me checking in with me—we tend to begin to feel better and less hurt or angry when we are acknowledged, even if it's by ourselves.

Once I have checked in with myself and I've made sure that I'm okay, I'm NOW ready to make an apology.

And here's the key to making the actual apology: DON'T make your apology conditional, ever. No 'buts' or 'ifs' included please.

You should NOT say something like, "Honey, I know I was wrong in the way I handled that BUT you have to admit, you were wrong too...." It won't work and it defeats the entire purpose of what we are trying to do here. The main problem with it is that you'd be trying to do the other person's work of apology FOR THEM, which doesn't work. In other words, you'd be saying TOO MUCH.

Instead, stick with, "Honey, I know I was wrong in the way I handled that. I'm sorry."

And Stop. At least for now.

Again, STOP. In my experience, people often 'panic' and fail to Stop.

In fact, a large number of the interpersonal conflicts I've been privy to could have been resolved in a faster and more Emotionally Competent manner had the participants known when to stop talking. People often make an excellent initial point only to undermine themselves with more words.

Don't worry about feeling that you haven't gotten a proper chance to justify or to defend yourself. You can ALWAYS have more conversations about the particular topic later on.

In fact, I like to use the phrases, "The game is never over.", and, "Life's a long race, not a short, so take it easy."

Don't panic.

Let yourself feel the weight of your words AS WELL AS the weight of your SILENCE when you Stop talking. Learn to deliberately Stop and to feel the power in that adult decision to Stop.

This is the weight that the other person will feel too, and with it you will have a chance of passing by their defensiveness and automatic reactions, and entering their heart with your apology.

Remember that the quality of your interactions with others depends not just upon your WORDS, but also upon your BEHAVIOR, which includes Restraint.

So if, while apologizing, you display a sense of agitation, anger, impatience, or insincerity, the other person's defensiveness will rise like a brick wall right in front of you and you'll be shut out—and so will your apology.

So be calm and poised: Let yourself feel centered and at peace. Only YOU can account for how you are feeling and behaving at any given time. Don't blame or shame and try not to be passive aggressive.

And, above all, don't get discouraged by the difficulty of all this.

I'd say that out of every one hundred attempts, I probably get this whole thing right maybe fifty or sixty times—and I do this for a living(!), so don't feel too horrible when you mess it up, and never give up.

The game is never over.

CHAPTER 31

EMOTIONAL FAT ON THE BONE (Y)

Emotional Fat on the Bone is a term I use to describe emotional resiliency.

It represents our ability to handle our lives with as much emotional competence as possible, as well as our ability to live as true adults instead of adult-appearing children.

Emotional Fat is like insulation or a buffer between your raw nerves and the world around you: the more Emotional Fat on the Bone, the better.

To borrow from our animal cousins for a moment, one of my Labrador Retrievers has a LOT of Emotional Fat on the Bone.

Low flying airplane over the yard? No anxiety for him.

Strange person walking up to us? He gives them the benefit of the doubt.

Changes in routine or food? He deals with it in stride.

My sometimes less-than-competent reactions or behaviors towards him? He forgives me, then we move on.

Multiple tasks in a row? He takes them on one by one until they're done.

How much Emotional Fat on the Bone do you have?

Here are some ways to tell, (incidentally, this list is by no means meant to make you feel badly if you find yourself lacking in Emotional Fat on the Bone, because the point is that we can always grow some more as we get better at living life):

1. How long does it take you to anger or lose control?

Less than a minute=very little Emotional Fat vs. hardly ever lose it=LOTS of Emotional Fat

2. What TYPES of situations can make you lose it or become angry?

Most situations=very little Emotional Fat vs. extreme situations=LOTS of Emotional Fat

3. How quickly, during a conversation, do you talk negatively or about negative things?

Within a few sentences=very little Emotional Fat vs. hardly ever, or not for a long time=LOTS of Emotional Fat

4. How much does it take to make you extremely anxious?

Everything makes me anxious=very little Emotional Fat vs. I tend to remain calm=LOTS of Emotional Fat

5. Do you hold grudges?

Yes, all the time, and for long periods of time=very little Emotional Fat vs. hardly ever=LOTS of Emotional Fat

6. How hard is it for you to trust people?

I don't trust people or their motivations=very little Emotional Fat vs. I start out trusting and let them prove me wrong=LOTS of Emotional Fat

7. How long can you focus on something without getting distracted?

Seconds=very little Emotional Fat vs. as long as needed=LOTS of Emotional Fat

8. How much does it take for you to become distracted?

The wind blowing=very little Emotional Fat vs. I am very focused when I need to be=LOTS of Emotional Fat

9. How much does it take for you to become overwhelmed?

More than one thing on my mind or getting interrupted overwhelms me=very little Emotional Fat vs. it generally takes a lot to make me feel overwhelmed=LOTS of Emotional Fat

10. How much patience do you have with people?

People are idiots=very little Emotional Fat vs. A LOT of patience=LOTS of Emotional Fat

11. How much does it take to frighten you or to make you feel threatened?

I feel frightened or threatened most of the time=very little Emotional Fat vs. I usually feel pretty secure= LOTS of Emotional Fat

12. How adventurous are you?

Not very=very little Emotional Fat vs. pretty darn adventurous if it interests me=LOTS of Emotional Fat

13. Do you like challenges and new things, or do you prefer things to remain the same?

I always prefer the status quo to change=very little Emotional Fat vs. I welcome change when it seems appropriate or advantageous=LOTS of Emotional Fat

14. How much of the time would you tend to take things personally?

I ALWAYS take things personally=very little Emotional Fat vs. I usually DON'T take things personally=LOTS of Emotional Fat

Having just given you all of these examples, let me encourage you by saying that, compared to the Labrador Retriever I described earlier, I have VERY little Emotional Fat on the Bone—so don't feel too badly.

In fact, the day I realized this was quite a wake-up call for me. Here was a dog that actually conducted himself in a more adult-competent manner in his life than I sometimes did in mine!

The level of Emotional Fat we have is a characteristic which is dependent upon two factors: one is our genetic, inborn temperament; the other, our upbringing and parental influences.

I have met people with excellent inborn temperaments, but who had overly-anxious or aggressive parents, and who therefore turned out to have about average levels of Emotional Fat on the Bone.

On the other hand, I've met people with significantly less genetic gifts, but who were exposed early on to one or two caregivers with lots of Emotional Fat on their bones. The result? Again, average degrees of Emotional Fat.

For most of us, we probably have somewhat average genetic temperament gifts (some of us are a bit on the anxious side, others a bit more aggressive, some maybe more easily distractible, etc.)

What this means is that we must all absolutely MAXIMIZE our genetic potential by practicing what I call adult emotional competency skills. To get you started, you can read about my REALADULTS acronym elsewhere in this book, where each letter of REALADULTS stands for an emotional competency skill.

The more we practice these skills in our lives, the more we will be able to leverage our inborn temperaments to create Emotional Fat, and the more we'll have to offer our children as well as the greater world around us.

Chapter 32

The Lid and the Boiling Pot (K)

Have you ever felt frustrated, helpless, ineffective, or downright dumb when trying to manage your adolescent child?

Some time ago, in my book Cobwebs and Ugly Wallpaper, I likened the idea of parents dealing with adolescents to trying to keep a lid on a boiling pot.

The upshot was that teenagers, and even some pre- and post-teens, are like boiling pots of water and that we the parents are like the lids that go on the pots: it is quite literally their job to push the limits with us--or, in other words, to try to throw the lid off of themselves as they boil through adolescence.

And when I say "throw off", I mean literally. They are trying to throw us off using any means necessary. It is their time to test us and to test the greater world around them in preparation for adulthood.

They might insult us or make innuendos to test our stability.

They might be ashamed of us or tell their friends that we are stupid and that we don't understand.

They might reject our guidance.

They might look at us or treat us with disdain.

They might not answer us at all when we talk to them and they might completely ignore us.

In other words, as the hormones rage and their cognitive abilities begin to develop in the direction of developing a sense of fairness, idealization, and logical thinking, they will act out righteously, like boiling pots set on throwing off their dullard lids.

It is our job to not be thrown off completely.

Trust me when I say that, your child, no matter how much he or she tells you to leave them alone, no matter how much they try to hide things from you or belittle your opinion--does NOT want you to give up on them. They want the lid to stay on. They NEED the lid.

Someone once told me that when he was a teenager his parents called the police on him one day and had him taken away, even though the responding police officers recommended against it. His parents had had enough. Another man shared that his parents ultimately gave up on monitoring his drinking and staying out late. Yet another told me about how his parents told him that he was allowed to smoke marijuana since THEY did it when they were his age.

What these three men also ultimately concluded was that they were disappointed in their parents, and that they later faced greater challenges and consequences in their lives than they felt they would have otherwise, had things been handled differently back then.

They felt, in sum, like they had succeeded in throwing the lid off the pot.

The point is that we will not necessarily WIN each battle with our adolescent children, but, ultimately, we can OUTLAST them.

And THAT'S our plan.

As long as you have this frame of reference, you will at least know that you are limiting the damage by realizing that the goal is not to make things nice and tidy and perfect with your teens; i.e. your kid may still experiment with drugs or alcohol or sex. BUT they probably will NOT do so to the extent they would have had you given up on them just because it seemed so impossible to win completely.

Your goal is to keep your cool--and your sound judgment--while they are at boiling.

Your goal is also to keep the RELATIONSHIP with them, no matter how ugly it may appear to become. Hang in there with them.

Also keep in mind that, by the time your child is a teenager, or even a pre-teen, you've already faced at least one other period of time when they've tested your limits and put you through some degree of h$ll.

Remember the 'terrible twos'?

Between the ages of 24 to 36 months of age, our children are experimenting for the first time with their independence from us on a smaller scale.

They needed limits back then, but they also needed our unconditional love, our empathy, our support, and our guidance, as they began to become more autonomous and as they made their first conscious (often horrible) decisions.

We now know that how we handle these initial 'decisions' of theirs can greatly impact their eventual personality development.

We don't want to over- or under-react. We want balance, a cool head, AND we want to keep our role as parent, guide, and teacher to them. (Notice how I DIDN'T say 'friend'--but that's for another discussion.) The LVAC technique works very nicely for this by the way, which you can read about elsewhere in this book.

In some ways, the situation with your adolescent is the same as when they were in those aforementioned toddler years; only now they are bigger and can potentially do more harm while going through this new phase.

But they'll still need your unconditional love and empathy, and--though they probably don't know it yet and would probably NEVER admit it if they did--they really DO need to NOT be able to throw the lid off the boiling pot.

CHAPTER 33

SEX AND MARRIAGE (M)

Let's talk about sex and marriage.

Typical scenario: a couple meets, "falls in love", has wonderful physical intimacy, and feels like they are in heaven; that they have found their mutual "soulmates".

Then it happens. Eventually, as the relationship continues, the sex decreases in frequency or perhaps even stops entirely. Maybe it takes years, maybe months, but it does happen.

Why?

Well, other than the fact that it's pretty normal for the frequency to decrease from the "good 'ole days" of the early relationship, there is something else at play for many couples as well and THAT'S what I want to talk about.

That is, they've lost the emotional connection.

Yes gentlemen, women tend to want to have physical intimacy (i.e. sex) when they are feeling emotionally intimate and connected first.

It is quite the contrary for most of us men who instead tend to feel the opposite way; that is, we feel emotionally closest when we've had sex. It's really just a difference in hardwiring. It's nothing personal, just ask God or evolution about it, whichever you prefer.

But, having just said that, the problem with many couples' sex lives has almost NOTHING to do with the hardwiring difference and it has almost EVERYTHING to do with the state of their emotional relationship.

If you recall from other parts of this book or from other things I've written, the definition of Emotional Credibility, or, E.C. for short, is a buildup of trust + liking the other person and wanting them around.

Well, by the time a couple comes to me about a problem with their sex lives, often they've already had a problem with their Emotional Credibility for quite some time. What this means is that they've lost the trust, and they really don't enjoy each other's company so much anymore.

And no, I'm not talking about the elusive "falling out of love", or, "we love each other but are just not in love anymore" thing. No, the concept of Emotional Credibility is a much more real, much more measurable concept than all that.

By the way, when I say "they've lost the trust", I'm not necessarily talking about the big trusts like fidelity, spending issues, substance abuse, lying, etc., although these are obviously very important issues and are the central point in some marriages.

No, for most of us, and in terms of Emotional Credibility trust, I'm talking about something I call "micro-trust"; i.e. will my spouse actually listen to what I'm saying without interrupting or trying to fix the situation or end the conversation. Will they become angry, dismissive, silly, shaming, blaming, or rejecting when I tell them something that's hard for me to talk about or that means a lot to me?

The fact is that, once the couple stops listening to each other, and validating each other's feelings and experiences (regardless of whether they're "right" or "wrong"), AND showing a real interest in each other, they've ceased to have any real trust (microtrust) in each other and they've also ceased to truly enjoy each other's company. Their sex lives will almost always suffer soon thereafter. It's just the way it works: loss of E.C. leads to loss of intimacy, both emotional and physical.

So, if you want to improve your marital sex life, don't start in the bedroom (well, you could start there, but that's a topic for another conversation.)

Instead, start by connecting with each other. Be a little bit "formal" with each other and behave yourselves like you did in the beginning of your relationship when you were just getting to know one another.

Don't take each other for granted, or assume that you really know each other already. GET to know each other: Listen, Validate, Ask questions, and save your Comments for last. (You can read elsewhere in this book about the LVAC technique, where LVAC=Listen, Validate, Ask, Comment.)

I'll often tell my patients that marital sex happens when we're not really paying attention:

If your spouse is chopping celery, ask if you can slice the tomatoes--that's sex.

If your spouse is angry, listen. Don't defend yourself right away, or get angry or leave--that's sex.

If your spouse is in some kind of trouble, support them as you learn about what's going on, don't punish or blame them right away--that's sex.

If your spouse needs you to think about them instead of yourself for right now, do it--that's sex.

If you know something your spouse needs or likes and you do it without waiting for them to ask and without getting angry if they don't immediately thank you--that's sex.

If you normally would never tell your spouse something but you take a risk and tell them anyway--that's sex. (And if you're the spouse hearing it and you don't immediately judge, dismiss, get angry, shame, blame, etc., that's sex too!)

I think you get the picture.

Marital sex is for true, emotionally competent adults, so follow these guidelines and put the sex back into your marriage!

CHAPTER 34

ENGAGEMENT IN YOUR LIFE (Y)

Are you truly engaged in your life? Meaning, do you feel a degree of fulfillment and a general feeling of being 'in sync' with yourself, your interests, and what you value?

What I'm also talking about here is the LACK of feelings of emptiness, chronic uncertainty or confusion, tension, anxiety, or distraction MOST of the time.

In my practice I often talk about "The Bicycle of Life", in which there is a Work Wheel and a Love Wheel. Roughly speaking, the theory goes like this: To live a truly fulfilling life, you must have some sense of the following four things about yourself-

1) what you like

2) what you don't like

3) what you want

4) what you don't want

In my practice, I call the sum of these four things your True Self.

With me so far?

Now, if your life reflects these four things--at least at some level--then you are living a life that is in line with your True Self and you will have more joy, more energy, less depression and anxiety, more creativity, and more emotional generosity with others, including your family. You will be truly engaged with your life.

If your life does NOT reflect the four components of the True Self in any way whatsoever, then you are "out of synch" with yourself, which leads to more conflict (both intra- and interpersonal), more anxiety and depression, less energy, and less of the real YOU available to the world.

Being disconnected from one's True Self can also lead to more acting out behaviors such as infidelity, inappropriate spending, drinking and drugging, excessive gambling and other risky behaviors, etc.--all in an attempt to fill the emptiness of the disconnect within yourself.

"So", you ask, "where does The Bicycle of Life idea come into play then?"

Glad you asked.

The concept of The Bicycle of Life, complete with its Work Wheel and Love Wheel helps us to conceptualize our lives in terms of how in-line we are with our True Selves--i.e., what we want, what we don't want, what we like, and what we don't like.

The Work Wheel includes all of your efforts in the "work" realm. These include any vocation (including full-time child-raising), avocation, hobbies, chores, etc., that can be considered part of your life's work.

The Love Wheel includes all of your relationships, including those with your children, your spouse, friends, neighbors, coworkers, family of origin, etc.

You may have noticed that there may be some overlap between the two Wheels, and that's fine.

Now, here comes the leap. Are you ready?

Through the Work Wheel and the Love Wheel of The Bicycle of Life, we have an opportunity to find out who we really are; in other words, we can find our True Selves.

Most of us lose touch with our True Selves somewhere in childhood, when our primary caregivers, try as they might, failed to use an LVAC type of approach in raising us (where, as you'll see in other parts of this book, LVAC stands for Listen, Validate, Ask, and Comment last), thereby, unfortunately, helping us to disconnect not only from them, but also from our True Selves at a very young age.

It's simple really: If you take a child and Comment back to him before Listening, Validating, and
Asking some open ended questions about where they were going with their thoughts or feelings, you replace THEIR developing True Selves, with your own immediate reactions via your Comments. Thus, you short-circuit the full expression of their thoughts or feelings to you, but, more importantly, to THEMSELVES. After a steady diet of this treatment, the child loses a sense of what THEY were thinking or feeling and with it, eventually, a sense of what THEY want, don't want, like, or don't like.

They lose THEMSELVES.

True Self, gone.

Disconnect and emptiness, present.

Now, back to the Bicycle of Life: Thankfully--for both ourselves and our children--we have, as adults, these two tremendous SECOND opportunities (i.e. the Work Wheel and Love Wheel), to find, or RE-FIND our True Selves in order to live lives of full engagement despite our early childhood experiences with our primary caregivers.

So, remember, every experience you are negotiating in your "work" or "relationships" today is really all about YOU. You will come up against YOURSELF first in all of these things:

Trouble with your boss? Learn about what he/she is triggering in YOU and where it comes from.

Afraid of taking a chance on that project? Find out more about your fears and what they are really telling you about yourself.

Feeling a disconnect between yourself and your spouse? Schedule at least 15-20 minutes each evening just to talk with each other once the chaos of the day finally abates.

Chronically overwhelmed or angry with your kids? Chances are that these sticky points or "buttons" are the same ones your parents had with you (a topic I've covered elsewhere), so you never really learned how these situations were supposed to be negotiated appropriately. Try doing the opposite of what you normally would do, or watch how your spouse handles these situations after you share with them what's being triggered for you. (Fortunately, it's fairly uncommon that both spouses will have the exact same triggers with the kids, which means that while you may be vulnerable to acting inappropriately in a given circumstance, your spouse may not be--where one is weak, the other will thankfully be strong.)

Starting to date (online dating, offline dating, blind dating, etc.)? Remember that everything you are experiencing with your dates is really first of all about YOU. Instead of trying to second guess the other person and give them what you think THEY want by behaving or looking a certain way, focus on being honest with yourself and with them, and let the rest be up to your developing True Selves. It will either work out, or it won't, but have the courage and the conviction to allow yourself to be True.

Regarding this last example, it never ceases to amaze me how badly people want to appear to be a certain way when dating in order to "succeed" on the date or to "not get rejected". And with the advent and growing popularity of online dating this phenomenon has become even more patently observable. People will literally ask me how they should respond to emails and other materials in order to move forward and successfully negotiate a certain stage of the online dating ritual, so they can go on to the next step, as if it were a series of exams meant to prove some sort of minimum competency or certification.

I remind people--and I'm reminding you--that how you handle the questions and other interactions with a potential mate, and, in fact, how they feel about the questions themselves is what's most important: It's the process itself which can potentially bring us back to the True Self by making us explore our own feelings and reactions, not the outcome of the date.

We are supposed to, in a sense, use these experiences to learn about ourselves, more than we should worry about whether or not any particular person will want to be with us. It's the former that will lead to joy, and all the other things I described earlier that go with finding and living in-line with the True Self more than it is what particular mate we end up with.

So stay True to your Self, and use your experiences in the Work Wheel and Love Wheel of The Bicycle of Life to help you reconnect with it. In my opinion, that's the goal of a live well lived, and it will affect both you and those around you in profound ways as you experience for yourself--and eventually share--who you are really meant to be once the disconnect is healed.

Then, unlock the power of True engagement with your life and feel the surge of energy, creativity, tranquility, and assuredness that comes with it!

CHAPTER 35

THE DANGER OF MAKING GENERALIZATIONS (K)

Can you remember times when you've been so beside yourself with someone, so overwhelmed with disappointment in them or with anger towards them that you made a statement that begins like this: "You ALWAYS...", or, "You HAVE ALWAYS...", or, "YOU'RE ALWAYS..."?

Or, maybe it was more like, "You NEVER...[listen, care, understand, etc.]!"

Or, maybe you LABELLED the person with statements such as: "You are such a...!", or, "You'll never be...!"

I call these statements "generalizations" and they can be destructive not only to the relationship, but--and especially when used with children--to the other person's self-image and self-esteem.

For example, if I say to my child, "Put your bicycle back in the garage please.", but then I also add, "Geez, you never listen!", or, "Come on, I've told you a thousand times!"--now I've made a generalization which does two things: firstly, it tells them more about me and my own overwhelmed internal state than they need to know and therefore puts us at risk for role reversal, (i.e. having them take care of me emotionally instead of vice versa, since I'm the one freaking out), and, secondly, it "labels" them as a "never listener".

So in one fell swoop, I have lost some of their trust in me and in my ability to handle myself and to guide them in life (remember Emotional Credibility?), AND, at the same time, I have also begun to undermine their self-esteem and self-image--i.e., their subconscious view of themselves, which will have very powerful effects on them later on in life--all by labeling them.

The funny thing about acting out our pain on others in this way, (i.e. by making generalizations), is that it makes the other person ultimately trust us LESS and it also tends to make them act out MORE in reaction to our generalization. And they will often do so in ways directly related to the label we've given them.

So, for example, if we tell them that they never listen, guess what? They end up listening LESS.

If we tell them that they are a jerk, guess what? They end up acting more like jerks with us.

If we tell them that they ALWAYS do a particular thing which annoys or angers us...you get the gist.

What we need to remember is that when we turn a person into a generalization, we are effectively putting a separation between us and them. In other words, we are becoming more distant from them, not more emotionally intimate.

Think about it for a moment: If your tendency is to say things in a tone which is upsetting to me and all I do in return is to yell at you stating that you ALWAYS use that tone with me, what have I accomplished?

Maybe in the small minority of cases, you would learn that I don't like that tone and you'd change it, no questions asked. Fat chance though.

The majority of the time, you'd get defensive OR you'd pull away from me--and I'd get even more of that behavior from you because nothing really ever got resolved with my "generalization comment".

But if, instead, I focused on the present example of this behavior which bothers me (e.g. your tone), I am now simply pointing out your behavior to you in the present and what it does to me. I am not attacking you by labeling you or telling you how much you s@%k (insert popular adolescent or pre-adolescent word here--one which neither you nor I would EVER dream of using, of course.)

Make no mistake, when we generalize at somebody, we're attacking them. It is an attack more than it is a communication. We are frustrated or otherwise hurt by them, but we are not telling them in a direct, accurate way, and we are definitely NOT working through the issue with them in the present when we generalize.

And, assuming that they are a human being, they will likely react, and if it's a human of the little child variety, then they'll also internalize the generalization and--in short--it'll become part of who they eventually become as adults. It's true. And it's not good.

Don't believe it?

Well, try to suspend any disbelief you may have for a moment and hear me out.

When you are in the privileged position that I am in, meaning you are allowed to share in the stories of thousands of wonderful people each year, you learn that:

The fifty year old procrastinator was once a twelve year old child who was repeatedly LABELLED a procrastinator.

The forty-five year old expert at self-sabotage was repeatedly called a "screw up" as a child.

And, when it comes to marriage, you'll lose Emotional Credibility with the other person, which, as you might recall, equals trust + being liked by them and having your presence be desired by them.

So please, don't generalize with your loved ones--communicate with them instead. Stay in the present with the behavior that's happening right now, not in the past or the future.

CHAPTER 36

THE MARRIAGE PROBLEM (M)

What if a genie, in some fantasy world, told you that you HAD to jump off of a cliff? --BUT--before you did so you were told that there would be an interesting caveat. You could either fall ...OR...... FLY!?!

Yep, that's right, fly.

And let's also say that The Rule was as follows: If you could believe with all your heart that you could fly, taking a running start and going as fast and as confidently as you could go, pumping your arms and breathing as hard and as deeply as possible before you 'jumped', then, well, you'd fly! (By the way: Do NOT try this experiment at home!!!)

If, however, you resisted the jump with all your might, or you tried to avoid or to ignore it altogether, either from fear or from doubt—or both—then you'd fall.

Okay, now back to reality.

The problem with marriage is that it is just like the dilemma I've just described: that is, we're already married—we've 'jumped in'—so now SOMETHING is going to happen no matter what. We'll either fall or we'll fly.

So, we can either be proactive, have faith and courage, and pour energy into it so that we'll grow stronger in our marriages (i.e. fly), OR we eventually hurt each other, build up resentment, and maybe even emotionally and spiritually kill each other (i.e. fall).

There really is no in-between in this case: In marriage, as time goes by, we WILL either grow or we WILL get hurt, period.

I have yet to meet a couple who have lived together for any appreciable amount of time and who have not had one of these two outcomes, be it obvious or more subtle in each particular instance.

When we marry and commit to another individual long-term, we eventually get closer and closer to them: We enter their inner circle or their "emotional boiler room".

And as we get closer to one another, certain things are bound to develop:

Our reactions towards each other will change over the years.

Our attitudes and what we're willing to put up with will change.

What we thought was 'cute' or 'cool' about each other will change.

Our patience with each other will change.

Our feelings about each other, and how we view one another will change.

Our consideration of each other and our thoughtfulness towards one another will change.

That 'specialness' and those 'butterflies' will change.

And eventually, we're back to the cliff analogy, where we find ourselves either growing stronger and flying with each other

OR falling with one another as we make ourselves miserable and punish each other over time.

But—and have no doubt about it—either way things WILL develop and change.

To illustrate, picture a pottery wheel.

Now picture the wheel going around and around: Wherever you apply pressure with your hand, that is where you'll make a groove or change the shape of the piece.

Time is like the spinning pottery wheel. It doesn't stop. And wherever you apply 'pressure' (i.e. your behaviors, reactions, attitudes, etc.), THAT is where you'll form grooves and change the shape of things in your life, including in your marriage.

One way or another, it's gonna come.

You'll either charge off that metaphorical marital cliff in a deliberate and purposeful manner, with the energy and faith and the confidence to make it right and healthy and good, OR you'll be a passive participant and things will happen TO you.

Unfortunately, like in our story, we have no choice in marriage; it's one of those few truly black-and-white life scenarios.

From the day we say 'I do', we've set the wheel in motion.

What happens next really is up to us, but things WILL happen.

Things WILL change and develop one way or another.

We must either be proactive, and pour energy and intentionality into learning about how to deliberately make our marriages better, OR our marriages will merely happen to us.

And, trust me, one or the other WILL happen.

So, take heart, read all you can about how to grow in your marriage as well as how to grow your marriage, and make sure your spouse does the same thing.

Remember, one way or another, time WILL go by and you WILL either grow closer together or further apart, even if you think you can resist it.

As I said in my marriage book, there are three kinds of marriages:

1) the ones where we celebrate our Golden Wedding Anniversary (hurray!), but only because one person puts up with all the 'stuff' (to be polite) that the other person does, producing quiet (or not so quiet) resentment and maybe some depression and anxiety issues to boot

2) the divorces, and

3) the ones who are proactive, who question themselves and each other, who want to learn, and who want to grow both as INDIVIDUALS and as married couples

I want your marriage to be in that last category.

CHAPTER 37

HEALTHY SELF-ESTEEM (Y)

What does it mean to have a healthy self-esteem?

Ever wonder what a healthy self-esteem actually feels like?

These days, we regularly read about and hear about how to build our self-esteem and how to preserve our children's self-esteem in magazines, on television, on the radio, and in books.

I want to ask you to do something: Picture a time in your life when you really felt happy with yourself. I mean honestly, truly happy with you. Just you.

Not with a possession, not with a particular accomplishment, and not with a relationship; just with yourself.

Are there such moments for you in your life? If so, what were they like?

Being that I am a psychiatrist, people are often interested in my professional opinion as to whether or not I think that they are doing the right things or making the right decisions in their lives.

Sometimes the questions involve things that could affect a person's self-esteem in some way, shape, or form and whether or not there are any particular changes that need to be made in order to negotiate those things in the healthiest way possible.

For example, people have asked me if I thought it would be healthy for them to get plastic surgery—a "nose job", breast implants, tummy tuck, liposuction, etc.

Or, they might ask about gastric bypass surgery, hair replacement, or hair removal.

How about professional teeth polishing or veneers?

Should I lose more weight, gain more muscle, put lifts in my shoes?

Should I only wear certain colors or avoid others?

Dresses or pants?

Full suits or sport jackets?

And I don't mean to make the last few items sound trivial, because for some people, they really are not trivial at all.

The fact of the matter is, all of us, to some extent or another, have to negotiate a sense of self-security and self-esteem on a regular basis.

And many, many things can affect it, including failures, successes, relationship and financial status, work and family issues, etc.

Despite all this, let me simply say that you often have more leeway than you think regarding what is reasonably appropriate and what isn't when it comes to building or keeping up your self-esteem.

As long as you're not hurting yourself or anyone else, you can often—after appropriate research and professional consultation if it's a procedure you want done, or at least some open and honest discussion with a friend or family member if it's not—pursue options which may help you feel a greater sense of self-esteem by helping to address something that you've perhaps struggled with for a very long time.

Of course, nothing can replace the self-esteem that comes from a tranquil inner peace and an accurate sense of, and appreciation for, who we really are as individuals. That all comes from the inside.

But I also think it's wrong to judge ourselves or others too quickly when deciding to do things that make us feel good about ourselves, especially if no harm is being done, and if those things are very specific and we don't go overboard.

Yes, one can go too far with this and essentially become addicted to temporary quick fixes which never lead to lasting change. But my professional experience has mostly consisted of people who have made well thought out decisions allowing them to take charge of and change an aspect of themselves which they simply could not make peace with--often for their whole lives up to that point, and often preceded by much internal struggle, growth, and change in therapy first.

Some particular examples include those whose self-esteem was strongly affected by childhood anomalies like moles or birthmarks that they were exquisitely sensitive about despite therapy, or a lip or palate issue of the mouth, or a hair loss problem, severe scarring acne or other skin issues, or teeth problems.

Others have struggled all their lives with metabolism issues despite making significant psychological and nutritional progress. Some have had major body or health changes after giving birth or upon getting to a certain age—changes they could not make peace with no matter how hard or how long they've tried and despite positive and healthy interventions along the way.

I've seen permanent and lasting change in many who have addressed issues which they could simply not reconcile within themselves and their lives. I've seen them become better spouses, better parents, better workers, better neighbors, and just plain happier and more positive people.

These are the stories which give me pause and which make me ask myself: How much therapy would be required to make a small stone stop bothering me if it were in my shoe? (Answer: none!)

So if you're thinking of getting a procedure done or making a change—of addressing any particular aspect of your appearance, personality, or environment in any way at all—please make sure that you try to open yourself up and explore it a bit first. Choose people who would be empathetic with you but who would also point out the potential pitfalls or dangers in your plan.

And also be open to the hard work of trying to change how you feel about yourself from the inside first, for that is where our self-esteem ultimately comes from regardless of what else we do on the outside.

CHAPTER 38

THE EMOTIONAL WEATHER SYSTEM AROUND YOU (M)

What sort of emotional weather system do you carry around with you?

When you come home from work, do you bring in clouds or sunshine with you to your family?

Do you regularly complain, berate others, act belligerently, fuss about, tell people what they're doing (or have done) wrong, or tell everyone how exhausted and frustrated you are all the time?

Or do you try to restrain some of these things and focus on being present with your family (including your spouse) when you're at home with them

Each of us has the power to bring the people around us down, or, on the other hand, to lift them up; to help them feel connected and alive--it all depends upon the emotional weather system we bring.

If, for example, I allow myself to "let loose" on my family all of the pain and conflict of a given day or a given week, then I'm coloring their sky with dark clouds. And, because of this, I'm also losing Emotional Credibility with them, which is the same thing as saying that I lose the trust + the likability factor with them.

That's because a funny thing about we human beings is that we unconsciously "reference" each other even before we even realize consciously that we're doing it.

Let me explain: When I think of Sally, my subconscious mind will, automatically and before I even have a chance to know it consciously, make a quick overall assessment of her Emotional Credibility. My subconscious will then either reference her to the good, so to speak, or it will reference her to the bad, depending on the result of that instantaneous assessment.

You can think of it as my immediate gut reaction to Sally.

Now it's true that sometimes we form a gut reaction to someone without even knowing them, and this is sometimes called a "transference reaction"; i.e. they trigger something in us on a subconscious level from past people we've known or experiences we've had.

However, we are talking about something very different here. The idea of coloring someone's sky with darkness or sunshine (i.e. with our emotional weather system) is a more controllable, CONSCIOUS phenomenon because it involves learning to deliberately recognize and modify our behavior.

We can actually choose to restrain our momentary misery or upset instead of letting it immediately--and often inappropriately--bleed all over everyone else around us, so to speak.

And the most powerful part of this concept is that it's contagious.

In other words, if I act out my pain by being miserable around you, then you will, in turn, most likely take on my emotional weather system and pass it along to the next person. But even if you don't take it on and pass it along directly, you will, at the very least, absorb it and it will affect your mood, self-esteem, sense of tranquility, focus, etc.

On the other hand, if I demonstrate some degree of control over myself and, at least for the moment, restrain myself, then you'll feel differently in my presence since the emotional weather system over us will be generally brighter.

Maybe you'll actually have a chance to tell me about how YOU'RE feeling. Or maybe you can tell me something about your day, or about the kids, your project, etc.

The point is, I won't have ruined the chance of connecting with you and building Emotional Credibility with you by casting a dark emotional weather system over your head with my negativity, anger, misery, or criticism.

Something I call the spirit of LVAC in my book, LVACNation!, (where LVAC stands for Listen, Validate, Ask, and Comment), means that we approach other people in our lives with a sense of restraint so that we can learn more about them.

The LVAC stance or spirit is a position of inquiry, not of Comments. We learn to Listen, then to Validate peoples' feelings, before we might Ask some open-ended, conversation producing questions, holding our Comments for last.

When we come in all negative or angry, with guns-a-blazin', we are Commenting first instead of Listening first. We are in what could be perceived as an aggressive, controlling, self-centered stance instead of an LVAC stance or spirit. We are telling the other person that we are the center of attention, not them, and not anybody or anything else but ourselves.

We come across as insecure, unsettled, agitated. And we are coloring their sky and their emotional weather system with dark clouds.

Try to practice checking in with yourself and your emotional weather system BEFORE you engage your loved ones.

We have to try to keep in mind that it's ultimately up to us how people automatically reference us when they think of us: will it be dark clouds and doom and gloom or sunshine, competence, and hope?

CHAPTER 39

TRUST BY THE POUND (Y)

If you've ever watched the popular show THE OFFICE, introduced to me some years ago via a DVD box-set gift from my parents-in-law, you might remember a particularly funny episode when Dwight tells a co-worker that he buys his clothes 'by the pound'.

Now Dwight, who is of Amish heritage in the series, makes it no secret that he grew up on a farm and that he was raised with some of the same practical, minimally materialistic, no-frills ways of his ancestors: thus, clothes by the pound.

Just give me the right materials, says Dwight, crafted into some solid, quality clothes, and I'll buy them by the pound with no need for further details other than fit.

So, what's all this got to do with trust?

The other day I was talking with someone about their relationship, and, more specifically, about how one might go about choosing a good spouse to build a life with; in other words, what to look for "by the pound".

I remember telling this person that I myself would look for 'trust by the pound'.

Another way of saying this is that I wouldn't necessarily look for the usual niceties and idealized behaviors that we've come to expect and to even thrive on early in our relationships.

(Remember the 'idealization phase' that I talk about in my marriage book?)

No, you can keep your gifts, your sweet tone with me, your doing little things for me, etc., because although these things are nice, I also know that they are often fleeting, temporary, and only available during the initial, idealization phase of a relationship: I know that these characteristics that we show in the beginning often have very little to do with who we actually are in the long run.

You know how it goes: We are on our very best behaviors and we are also willing to overlook many things (many things!) in the very beginning, when we are 'in love' or when we think we've found our 'soul mate'.

For me, when I say, 'trust by the pound', I'm thinking about how I want my children to choose someone when it comes time; I'm thinking about core characteristics of a person's character and personality.

I'm looking for the heavy stuff, not the window dressing. I'm looking at whether the person is a cup which can hold water, or more of a chronically 'leaky' cup: Do they know (or want to learn) how to live a good life, connected to others and to their work in the world?

Are they willing to question themselves and to grow?

Are they consistently empathetic in their behaviors towards others? Do they seek to truly understand, listen, and learn? Do they display compassion? (And not just in the beginning and not just when they stand to gain something immediately in return.)

Do they seem engaged in their lives--in their relationships and in their work and other activities?

When they say, "I love you", do they already have or are they at least trying to build the emotional competence needed to back these words up? Can they commit, and do they really understand commitment?

Looking for trust by the pound doesn't mean looking for perfection. No one among us is perfect, and we've all made our mistakes and have hopefully learned from them. It also doesn't mean looking for that initially great behavior or attitude in someone which eventually fades and goes away when their true colors eventually come out.

Let me observe someone for a day or two and I can generally tell you how much trust you can safely have in them without getting severely hurt or ending up feeling completely betrayed when they 'change': I'll be looking for how they conduct themselves with the wait staff at a restaurant. I'll be looking for how closely they follow through on what they tell people they are going to do. I'll be looking for how honest they seem to be with themselves and how at peace they appear to be in their own skin.

I'll also, and perhaps most importantly, be looking for their willingness to learn and to grow as a person.

If there's one thing my work has taught me over the years it's admiration and affection for the people I've met who are willing to learn about themselves, even when the things that they are learning aren't necessarily to their liking.

I've found that these are the people who, in the long run, you can most likely 'trust by the pound'.

CHAPTER 40

HOW BEING STUCK CAN CAUSE OTHER PROBLEMS (Y)

Ever been stuck in your life?

You know, stuck, as in, "damned if I do, damned if I don't".

For instance, maybe you've had to make a decision about something when all the options seemed somewhat unacceptable to you on some level or another.

When we find ourselves in a quandary because all of the available options seem unacceptable to us, perhaps because they cause us anxiety, fear, shame, etc., then we are officially 'stuck'.

And here's the very practical, very real problem with being stuck like this: we might ultimately find ourselves acting out in order to get 'unstuck', thus making the situation worse.

So, for example, if I have a financial problem but every potential solution engenders fear or anxiety in me (like beginning by discussing it with my wife, for example), then to get 'unstuck' I might just blow all the rest of the money, or somehow make myself too sick to work, or I might even get myself fired—all of which will obviously make things much worse for me.

My feeling of being stuck just made things worse for me by producing acting out behaviors which 'solved' (really made worse in actuality) the problem: kind of like throwing a hand grenade into a sock drawer in order to clean it up.

Some people might act out sexually by having an affair, or with drugs or alcohol, or with bad business decisions or procrastination: Whatever the method used, the acting out process represents the subconscious mind 'solving' the 'unsolvable problem' for us, albeit in a destructive way. This is the best the subconscious mind can do to solve the problem of being stuck.

So the bottom line is this: If we don't consciously come up with or work through some sort of reasonable, acceptable solution to the problem making us feel 'stuck', then our subconscious will 'solve' it for us, and not in a productive way.

Going back to our first example, if a couple is having financial problems but say the husband is worried or fearful about sharing this with his wife and feels increasingly stressed out, stuck, and alone. Now let's say that eventually he begins to confide in another woman. One thing leads to another and they eventually have an affair. Now, of course, problem solved!—No marriage, no problem! Not good.

Or, let's say a wife is completely stressed out but continues to try to hold it all together for fear of disappointing or upsetting her husband but then finds herself increasingly alone in her struggle and in her suffering. What can happen subconsciously to 'solve' the problem? Again, acting out with addictive behaviors, anger with the spouse or kids, 'retail therapy', affairs, etc., are all possibilities.

The key is to begin to recognize when we are feeling stuck, which means recognizing when a problem seems 'unsolvable' to us.

The next step is to get some help.

Talk it out with someone, because, more often than not, there is a viable solution--and it's often one that we haven't come up with ourselves because of the strong emotional load that the original problem holds for us.

By talking it out with someone else, we can often get a clearer, more objective view of the possibilities for a healthy resolution to the situation.

CHAPTER 41

THE EXTRAORDINARY SPIRIT OF CHILDREN (K)

I am writing this because I want to help remind us just who our children really are, because sometimes we forget.

I'm purposely using the word extraordinary here to describe the spirit of our children and here's why: From the moment they are born, our children want nothing from us but our love and our focused attention.

Our LOVE and our focused ATTENTION. That's all they want from us, and, to me, that's pretty darn extraordinary.

They are not born asking for money or the keys to our cars. They were not born to manipulate or denigrate us or stress us out. And they were NOT born by their own free will.

As a parent, I know just how hard it really is to give these two things—love and attention—consistently to our children, especially the latter. In fact, I sometimes tell my patients who are parents (with tongue in cheek) that the real meaning of 'Attention Deficit Disorder' is the DEFICIT of attention from us to our children.

Life is hard, and just seems to get harder and busier all the time. The reality is that, for many of us, our kids are at times made to feel like an unwanted distraction or interruption from whatever else is going on--things which are just too 'important' for them to be interrupting.

Some examples include:

-work stuff

-marital problems

-anxiety or depression issues

-home improvement projects

-outside commitments/organizations

-hobbies

-other relationships (including parents and siblings)

-bills and finances

-habits and/or addictions

-other 'adult matters'

-ANYTHING OTHER THAN THEM

In my book, Don't Get Married! (Unless You Understand A Few Things First), I talk about how the time and energy we give to our spouses is not supposed to be "left-over" time and energy, but, instead, "prime" time and energy.

This same idea also holds true for our children, and, in some ways, even more so.

As a father, no matter how rushed, busy, worried, overactive, engaged, or distracted I get, I try to always remind myself that my children never asked to be born and that I owe them for making my dreams of becoming a father to them come true.

I WANTED them. And I still do.

It's just that we parents have to remind ourselves of that and of the remarkable, extraordinary spirit and transient, magical presence of these little humans in our lives.

The fact is that our children, especially the little ones, literally live for and because of us. Science has taught us that human babies are perhaps the most dependent baby creatures on Earth. Without us, they wouldn't make it very far.

But, leaving sheer physical survival alone for a moment, let's instead focus upon the emotions and spirit of our kids. They observe us and they study us.

In fact, someone once told me that our kids are watching us even when we are least aware of it.

When one of my children comes to me to show me something or to tell me something, a lot is going on right there: EVERYTHING with kids, especially little kids, is a metaphor for something bigger.

In fact, children speak and act in a metaphorical language all their own.

One day, my son, who was 7-years-old at the time, said to me: "Dad, you're not the most important person here." I had been talking to my wife about something that moved me emotionally the previous day and my young son overheard some of it.

Now, he hadn't heard much (by my design), but he heard enough to know that daddy was a little upset. Translation to the child's spirit: dad's upset, so he's really not with ME, but with HIMSELF right now.

No judgments were made, no criticisms. But he had perceived something very important, and he was right.

What I left out was that he was about to get on the school bus and he needed my support and encouragement. He needed me to focus on HIM for that moment.

He was simply pointing out the truth to me, in his own, metaphorical, innocent, child-way.

We need not be defensive about or feel put upon by our children's need to have us be focused on them, especially when they are young.

Anything, even deliberate or necessary things, which take our internal, heart-focus away from them when they need us is noticed immediately by them--right now subconsciously, but later on they will know it more consciously in the form of thinking that they need us less or perhaps even not at all. It almost becomes a sour grapes type reaction, as in, "I never could have you anyway, so I don't really need you now."

In reality, kids really do (and should) need their parents for a good long time. It doesn't matter if I am ninety and my kids are in their fifties. If I'm still somewhat competent mentally by then, they'll still, on some level or another, need me as their parent: there is no end to this job.

Now, getting back to that word 'extra-ordinary' from the title of this chapter: the reason I used this word is because children have the remarkable power to take on blame for our shortcomings or emotional immaturity as parents. This means that if I systematically ignore them or allow myself to be constantly distracted from them, they will be more than happy to try to NOT notice the truth of what's going on.

In other words they will REPRESS the fact that I'm not paying much attention or giving much time to them, (picture the classic reading the paper or watching T.V. while saying,

"Uh-huh, yeah, uh-huh...."), AND they will feel the disconnect from me, but they won't really know what it is.

Chances are they will take on the disconnect themselves and they will also BECOME disconnected FROM themselves: that's right, our disconnect from them becomes their own disconnect from themselves.

What they won't be able to do is to say (and truly believe), "Oh well, dad's just busy and has a lot on his mind right now, but he really does love me and he wants to be with me"--because that's just not the full story. The full story is that we the parents are already disconnected from ourselves because of our own, similar, childhood experiences with our disconnected caregivers. It's a repeating cycle.

And by not stopping the cycle with our kids, we are not only passing along the disconnect to them--making them vulnerable to all sorts of acting out behaviors later on in order to fill the void left by that disconnect--we are also losing an opportunity to heal the disconnect within ourselves by doing for them what our caregivers did not do for us: i.e., we could just stop what we are doing and pay attention to them.

To illustrate, consider my "Two Minute Rule": no matter what your kid (or anyone else) is wanting to say to you, you can ALWAYS stop and listen for just two measly minutes.

I mean, unless someone literally drops in front of you and you have to immediately do CPR, you've almost definitely got two lousy minutes, right?

So let's us parents remember a couple of things: first, that we've almost always got those two minutes to give, which, to our credit, will seem like two HOURS to them; and, next, that our kids are here because we chose to make them which means that we owe them.

Make a special effort with them which befits their special (extra-ordinary!) place in your heart and in your life.

CHAPTER 42

UNCONDITIONAL LOVE VS. UNCONDITIONAL POSITIVE REGARD (M)

There is a big difference between Unconditional Love and Unconditional Positive Regard.

Unconditional Love is what parents are supposed to give to their children. It refers to the fact that since the child is not yet ready to be fully responsible for their behaviors, they can bring to the parent their emotional "poopie diaper" and the parent will help clean it up and will still love them. It is to be expected. That is Unconditional Love.

In other words, children should not have to censor themselves or "pre-clean" before going to their parents. It's the parents' responsibility to take their child as they come, especially when they are still young, and to deal patiently and with adult competence with whatever the child brings to them.

Unconditional Positive Regard, on the other hand, is what PEERS can give to each other. It means "benefit of the doubt". It does NOT mean Unconditional Love, because, unlike children, we adults ARE supposed to be responsible for our behaviors towards one another. (In fact, Unconditional Positive Regard is one of the ten adult competence skills in my acronym REALADULTS, which you can find elsewhere in this and my other books.)

You see, if I bring you, my PEER, my emotional "poop" and you feel obligated or forced to put up with it or to "clean it up" time and time again, it will eventually get pretty old. You will eventually resent me, as you become more my parent or babysitter than my peer. Put another way, I will lose Emotional Credibility with you, which, as you may recall, equals trust + likability.

The problem is that we often expect, no, we DEMAND Unconditional Love from our peers, (meaning our spouses), rather than Unconditional Positive Regard. We wish to be able to behave impulsively, without restraint, and to treat them any way we want to at any given moment, but still expect infinite understanding, patience, and immediate forgiveness. (Sounds an awful lot like poopie diaper cleanup, no?)

In other words, we subconsciously want them to be our perfect, all understanding and all forgiving parent, while we are the helpless victim child. Unfortunately, this is just not realistic in adult peer-to-peer relationships like marriage, and it leads to hurt, disappointment, and resentment, as well as both emotional and physical disconnect in the relationship.

In fact, the reason I came up with the term Unconditional Positive Regard in the first place is that it is something we adults CAN reasonably give to one another on a day-to-day basis without creating disconnect and resentment--it's something we can work with.

With Unconditional Positive Regard, we are responsible for our behaviors. This means that when we behave in a less than Emotionally Competent manner (i.e. with outbursts, acting out behaviors, lack of follow through, devaluing or belittling the other person, using a bad tone or malicious sarcasm, lying, having ulterior motives or manipulating, being selfish, etc.), we are willing to accept feedback and to correct these behaviors in order to preserve the connection between us. (Ever wonder where all the sex goes in so many marriages? It goes right where all the Emotional Credibility and emotional connection went—away!)

Unconditional Positive Regard also means that adult peers try to give each other the benefit of the doubt. It says that when you are mean or less that considerate with me I won't immediately jump down your throat or become defensive or angry right away, however, as I described above, I WILL point out your behavior to you and perhaps even what I would rather have from you. Your job is to then listen to my feedback and to use it to continue to grow into your most Emotionally Competent adult self.

Unconditional Positive Regard is an active, dynamic process between two adults, neither of whom are perfect reference points for mental health, but both of whom are willing to learn from each other's feedback.

As some of you have heard me say, "we are all just somebody else's messed up kid", so why should you expect yourself and your spouse to be perfect adults or parents to one another, or, on the other hand, to put up with bad behavior from each other, especially if the goal is to try to preserve the connection between you as peers and not build up the resentment that eventually causes marital disconnect--both physical and emotional?

Use Unconditional Positive Regard to say to your spouse, "Hey, I'm not your parent and you're not my helpless victim child. I will give you the benefit of the doubt here to explain your behavior, and then I'll tell you what I think about it so we can come up with something better for ourselves and for our relationship."

If you don't learn to talk like this to one another, you'll just get defensive instead, or you'll eventually pull back and withdraw from each other; nothing will ever get resolved or worked through and your relationship will grow more distant and less emotionally and physically intimate as time goes on.

If, on the other hand, you DO try to talk like this, you will be building up a customized, extremely valuable relationship with the other person; one in which you can each improve yourselves using the other person's Unconditional Positive Regard, along with their observations and feedback, as tools for personal growth.

Remember, adult peer-to-peer relationships, and especially marital ones, are really about OURSELVES. We grow within the relationships we have with other people and we learn about ourselves as we go through the difficult, often gut-wrenching work of ironing out the issues we have with one another in an honest, open-minded, optimistic, and exploratory manner.

Chapter 43

How to Help Somebody Calm Down (Y)

We've all been involved in heated, tense interactions: sometimes it's been with a stranger or an acquaintance, other times with a spouse or child. What's most remarkable to me about these moments is how easy it is for us to get sucked into behaving badly.

We can get defensive or even outright offensive, especially if emotionally triggered by what the other person is saying.

The best thing to do in these situations is to focus on de-escalating the situation rather than on escalating it further:

Husband: "Did you get a chance to pick up dinner?"

Wife: "No, I've just been too busy today, so you're gonna have to deal."

Husband: "Whoa, what the h*ll is that!?!"

Wife: "You're always expecting me to be responsible for feeding this family. I have a job too you know!"

Husband: "Well if you weren't so busy texting your girlfriends all day and calling your mother, you'd get out of work sooner and get dinner on the table!"

Wife: "You know what? Go to H*ll!! You don't appreciate anything I do around here and you never even get you're a*@ home on the weekends instead of going out fishing with your buddies or playing in your stupid softball league! Your kids never even get to see you!!"

And on and on it goes.

What you're seeing here is a whole lot of pent up resentments on both parts in all those attacks that's now getting acted out. People are always ready to be defensive or offensive with one another. We often carry with us many resentments, whether we know about them consciously or not, about various hurts and injustices in our lives from childhood through to the present day.

It pays, therefore, to know that no matter what the argument or disagreement is about, you'll always be better off focusing on de-escalating rather than adding fuel to the fire. Otherwise, in their eyes, you'll be just another "jerk" in a long line of jerks and you will instantly become the new focus of their resentments.

It's just human nature: If you're upset and you try to speak to someone and all they do is fight you back or act defensively with you, you will likely turn your anger towards THEM and they will become the focus of your resentment, anger, and perhaps even rage.

So start by listening.

Remember, if you don't listen first, you will automatically subconsciously get grouped in with all of the other people who haven't listened to her in the past or who have wronged her somehow.

And who wants to voluntarily become part of that group? Not me.

One option is to follow my LVAC® mnemonic: Listen, Validate, Ask, Comment.

Step 1: Listen to what the other person is saying; don't interrupt them.

Step 2: Try to Validate what they are trying to say. Seldom is it impossible to do this. You don't have to agree with them necessarily in order to validate their feelings anyway.

Step 3: Ask them some open-ended questions which will help them talk more so that they can narrow down just what it is that's bothering them. Many people need to start broadly and even angrily (or some other emotion) and need a chance to first say whatever's on their mind. After listening and validating, asking some open-ended questions and not commenting right away will help them process further their thoughts and emotions.

Step 4: Save your Comments for last, if they're needed at all at that point. Often, the most valuable part of the interaction was the Listening, the Validation, and the Asking.

So, the next time someone is telling you something, practice LVAC and avoid putting yourself in the direct line of fire. But seriously, you'll also help them feel better, and they'll like and trust you more.

CHAPTER 44

WHAT LEGACY WILL YOU LEAVE? (K)

The word legacy is probably about 600 years old. It usually means something we pass on to someone else, often after we're gone and often to future generations.

Sometimes, in my office, we end up talking about our mortality. We don't always get to it the same way, but we nonetheless do get there more often than we might expect.

Often, these sorts of conversations shed light upon a unique and powerful perspective: they allow us to consider our lives as a whole—a beginning part, a middle part, and an end part.

Do you ever think of your life as a whole like this? If you WERE to take this perspective with you into your everyday life with your spouse and your kids, as well as with the greater world around you, how would it change your behaviors and the choices you make? How would it change YOU?

Would it allow you to listen more and comment less? Would it remind you to be emotionally generous with people, and especially with your loved ones? Would it encourage you to challenge your fears and limitations so that you could learn more about who you are, your history, your talents and interests, and your destiny?

In his Meditations, Roman Emperor and warrior-poet Marcus Aurelius reminds himself (in fact chastises himself!) repeatedly that his life is already 'over' and that he needs to face that fact and behave accordingly. He understood the power of realizing the full spectrum of life: beginning, middle, and END. He knew that it was like a 'switch' that, once turned on, provided a sense of serenity and a certain freedom to focus, not on anxiety and doubt, but on the present.

This was a man who wrote to himself and for himself, and who never intended for a mass audience. He wrote in between battles, perhaps as he sat down on some beach on the edges of the Empire, resting his weary bones and nursing his wounds, while taking a break from planning the next push forward for his army.

How do we want to be remembered by our children and grandchildren? Do we want to leave them with a sense of courage and confidence? Or with fear, anxiety, and paralyzing self-doubt?

Do you know what makes a child feel more confident, settled, and personally powerful? When we stop for a moment and focus on them. When we listen to them. When we validate their feelings, no matter how uncomfortable we are about what they're saying. And when we ask them open-ended questions about themselves and what they are saying to us.

This approach of listening, validating, asking open-ended questions, and saving comments for last is called the LVAC ™ approach and you can learn more about it in other parts of this book as well as the website www.LVACNation.com.

When we try our best to behave like this with our kids, it empowers them and makes them grow strong from the inside. This means that you'll never have to worry (or you'll worry much less) that they'll grow up someday to be somebody's victim or a victim of circumstances that could have been avoided--because they ARE strong.

Imagine someone saying that they want their child to be strong and that's why they regularly say to them, 'buck up', 'suck it up', or 'deal with it'. The problem is, it's the exact opposite that's true. That is, if you want your child to eventually end up in a chronic state of self-doubt, conflict, and anxiety, then take the easy road and simply Comment at them, telling them to 'buck up', 'suck it up', or 'deal with it'. But if you want them to learn about themselves and not be unconscious about their feelings and who they are; if you want them to grow authentically strong, then Listen to them, Validate their feelings, and Ask them some open-ended questions before making those Comments.

Ditto goes for your spouse. Chances are that, like you, your spouse didn't get much LVAC growing up either, which means that not only do they not know about LVAC either, but that they are also starving for it just like you are!

One of the really remarkable things about marriage is that it's an opportunity for each of us to finally grow past our childhood limitations, traumas, fears, and anxieties by using our spouse to help us do so. I call it the Emotional Laboratory of Marriage for INDIVIDUAL growth. That is to say, my spouse and I use each other to grow and to heal from our respective childhood wounds. By using such tools as LVAC, and by cultivating a communication approach that emphasizes trusting each other enough to take risks by saying things we'd NEVER have been able to say as children, we help ourselves to grow past our childhood limitations and wounds.

Progress comes with each spouse becoming more and more in tune with their own emotions over time. When you employ LVAC with one another, you will help each other identify deeper, more repressed emotions over time. It's like built-in therapy with your spouse, only without the copayments!

Now back to the main point.

Obviously, if we are to live our lives with a sense of beginning, middle, and end, then we need to become better at observing and listening to ourselves and others.

When you are remembered, whether it is while you are still living and after you've just had a conversation with someone, or whether it is after your death, how will the person remembering you feel? Will they feel inspired and infused with goodness, strength, and hope? Or will they just say those things about you to be polite?

Whether we like it or not, from the time we are born two things happen:

1) the clock starts ticking,

and,

2) the record of our life begins.

Our actions, behaviors, decisions, and choices create our legacy, our record. And the people we have known—along with some we haven't—will have feelings when they think about us, one way or another.

And our spirit will live on in those feelings that they have.

CHAPTER 45

WHY WE MARRY WHO WE DO (M)

Picture a coin.

You know how it has two sides? Well, when we date someone, we see one side of the coin: Let's say, for example, that Sally likes the way Jonny opens the car door for her, and how he orders for her at the restaurant, and how he even pays the bill without hesitation or question!

Sally likes THIS side of the coin.

Now, let's take a look at the other side of the same coin: It turns out that, after several months together, Sally begins to notice that Jonny likes to have CONTROL over things, including HER things.

And here's the rub: in doing so, he helps put her into an emotional position of being a helpless, dependent little girl. She, of course, doesn't like this, even if she doesn't quite know why in her conscious mind.

The problem is that she DID like the way he "took control" early on; but she DIDN'T know that this came in package deal with the other side of the same coin, namely, putting her in the role of the helpless, dependent little girl.

To switch analogies for a moment: Sally liked the sun-roof option, but wasn't aware that she'd also be paying for the upgraded stereo and leather package as well.

Now let's look at Jonny's side of the story.

He just LOVED the fact that he was so liked and appreciated by Sally for the way he took "care" of her early on. But, as time went on, he began to resent how he had to always be the one to take the lead and to make all the decisions. He felt like he had another child instead of an adult partner.

At this point, let's step back for a moment so we can see just why they picked each other to begin with: As a child, Sally's mother and father had a lot of anxiety and worry about her. In fact, they overcompensated by making regular comments to her about the dangers of life and their worries about any given situation she was in at any given time.

Sally never really ever got a chance to test her mettle as she grew up, instead finding herself ever-increasingly accustomed to and comfortable in her role as a helpless, somewhat hopeless little dependent. And, best of all, her parents seemed to react better and less nervously when she STAYED in that role; it was more comfortable for THEM and Sally sensed that.

This role was not exactly healthy for Sally, but it's what she learned to become, the role she was trained to play starting in her childhood. Then, when she began dating as a young adult, something in her subconscious mind--that old childhood role she was used to playing--told her the type of person she'd be most comfortable with; someone who would help her continue this childhood emotional position of the helpless, frightened dependent. Enter Jonny.

Now Jonny's is an altogether different, but complementary, story.

Jonny's parents were constantly showing him how overwhelmed they were when he couldn't take care of himself or when he screwed something up. They always made it a point, either through their behavior or their words, to communicate to little Jonny how much they had to work to take care of him; how much trouble it all was to them. This, of course, was not fair to Jonny, but they never considered that: little kids are SUPPOSED to screw up and they're aren't meant to be able to take care of themselves at such a young age.

Nonetheless, Jonny grew up thinking that all the stresses and worries of his immediate situation could be prevented and that his parents could be made to be calm and tranquil and at peace if only he could develop the habit of predicting what would happen next so that he could CONTROL it and not add to their problems:

"Going out to eat? I already know what's good at this restaurant."

"Movie? I've got the reviews right here."

"Buying something? I've already researched it."

As long as Jonny was prepared and vigilant, his world (which originally meant his parents) would be okay.

Now fast-forward twelve years: When Jonny was allowed and encouraged by Sally to 'take control' early on in their dating, he was able to continue to act out on his childhood fears of his parents not being okay unless he made it so. Except now, instead of his parents, it was his girlfriend. He somehow felt 'comfortable' on a deep, subconscious level with Sally because with her he could resume his usual role, his comfortable role from childhood.

Healthy? No.

Comfortable and familiar? Yes.

Jonny was able to continue his childhood with Sally. You see, the weird thing is, had Sally protested his taking such control on their first date, they would NOT have felt mutually 'comfortable' with each other, and, therefore, they would very likely NOT have ultimately ended up together! And THAT's because what we initially 'like' and feel comfortable with when we are falling in love with somebody are the very things which later prove to be unhealthy repetitions of our childhoods!

So here we have a woman (Sally) who is prepared to continue her helpless role from childhood, together with a man (Jonny) who is happy to continue his "all powerful" childhood role.

Perfect, right?

Unfortunately, no.

Because, after a while, we humans begin to resent the ones who helped put us back into these unhealthy childhood roles and who helped perpetuate them. In addition, we usually don't consciously know that any of the stuff I just described is going on, so we don't get angry and resentful towards our original caregivers; instead, we get angry and resentful towards our spouses, who represent the latest edition of those original caregivers, and who therefore "inherit" all that unconscious resentment.

Seldom do we ever realize that our spouse is not the ORIGINAL person who hurt us; that they are not the ones who originally put us in these unhealthy positions. A spouse is simply someone who is pushing an already well-established button, for which they will ultimately inherit our rage.

In the end, we act out all that subconscious, stored up, childhood anger towards one another as we proceed to build up disappointment, resentment, and, sometimes, even contempt; and it's a long way back from contempt, as you might imagine.

We really have to remember that one's spouse is actually just somebody else's messed up kid who grew up--at least physical if not always emotionally!--and got married. The other thing to remember is that we have to help each other break out of the chains of our unhealthy childhood habits and knee-jerk emotional reactions by changing the ways that we behave towards one another which actually reinforce all that childhood stuff.

That's what marriage is really all about, and it's why I call marriage an Emotional Laboratory for each individual spouse's growth.

You see, there's an upside to all this: Since we've already gone through the trouble of selecting each other for exactly the "wrong", subconscious reasons, we've now got the perfect partners with whom we can now work on reversing those unhealthy childhood roles!

In other words, by inadvertently having our unconscious minds help us to choose our mates, we've also located and pinpointed each others' hurts from childhood. We found each other! I am now the one who hurts you the exact way your caregivers did and you hurt me the way mine did! Now, we can either continue to hurt each other by triggering and reinforcing the unhealthy childhood roles that we've each learned in our respective childhoods--thus continuing childhood together--OR we can help each other reverse those childhood positions and heal from them.

We are perfectly matched to either continue each other's childhood hurts or to reverse them!

CHAPTER 46

WHO IS IN THE WORDS THAT YOU SPEAK? (Y)

Can it be that it is really yourself that is in those words? Specifically, can it be that in your words are sometimes emotions that you either didn't know you had or that you're afraid to express more directly?

When you speak, how consciously aware are you of what you are saying and why you are saying it? Well if you're at all like most of us, there are times, and especially in close personal relationships, when you're not really very aware at all; or maybe you're only partially aware.

And, while we're at it, how good are you at identifying the feelings that you're having, the ones which are fueling your words? Again, like most people, maybe not so good?

I think that it is undeniable that, in general, when we speak, we are feeling something. Emotions fuel words. And I think that it is also undeniable that many of us aren't very good at identifying what we are feeling and, therefore, why we are saying what we're saying.

So one of our fundamental questions to ourselves when we speak should be: "Why am I saying what I am about to say?" In other words, "Who or what am I really talking about here?"

Another question I might ask is: "Why am I speaking?", or, "What is my intention here?"

For so many of us, speaking out loud involves multiple agendas, some conscious (known to us) and others subconscious (unknown to us), but we are usually only aware of the conscious agendas.

We often fail to realize the subconscious agenda or true feeling about what we are saying, but it does come out in the tone we use.

Conscious agenda: I'm going to tell my spouse that I need my ice scraper back for my car.

Subconscious agenda: Ever since my spouse lost (or broke) my key fob, I really don't trust him/her with my stuff.

Therefore, when you finally speak to your spouse about giving you back your stuff, you might say it with an accusatory or irritated-sounding tone because of the actual, subconscious agenda, i.e., that you're conflicted about trusting them.

Or, how about this one (conscious agenda): "I really don't think we should go to your family's house this year for Christmas. It just stresses me out."

Subconscious translation (actual feeling): "YOU have been stressing me out and I'm not willing to deal with both you AND your family this year."

Your tone will likely sound annoyed, irritable, or accusatory, which your spouse will pick up despite your conscious-agenda-"words", and you'll be off to the races with yet another argument.

As you see, it's very important for us to study ourselves and what we are really feeling. And it's important to learn to recognize our emotional "derivatives"; in other words, the flavor, look, or sound of the subconscious agenda and tone of our words, based on feelings that we are having but are not fully aware of or acknowledging to ourselves.

So why don't we simply acknowledge our emotions to ourselves so that we can know them consciously and therefore find a way to communicate them more directly instead of indirectly and destructively? It's because somewhere in our lives, often in childhood, we learned to hide our emotions from ourselves, probably because of bad experiences when we DID express them, or when we saw a sibling express them; so we learned to just stuff them.

Of course, we don't just get rid of strong feelings permanently, so we are left with indirect communication that is based upon these repressed emotions. In other words, we speak, but do not realize what we are really saying.

So, the next time you find your mouth moving and words coming out, try asking yourself this very important question: What am I feeling right now?

This will serve you well in helping determine who (or what) is really in the words that you speak.

Chapter 47

Us Compared to Our Parents (K)

What do you think of when you think of your childhood with your parents? Many of us have become furious defenders of our childhoods and of our parents' approach to raising us. We say things like, "I had a GREAT childhood!", or, "My parents were the best!"

Of course we love them and rightfully so, but because of this fact we are also at risk of repeating some of the not-so-great aspects of the way we were parented with our own kids: Ever wonder why certain, particular things your kids do trigger you so quickly?

"Johnny, clean up your mess."

Silence.

"Johnny, don't you DARE ignore me when I'm talking to you!!!"

Now here's the thing: What if I were to tell you that your strong reaction to Johnny in the example I just gave might contain some important information about your own parents' response to YOU when you ignored or didn't hear them as a kid?

Sometimes, when we have an immediate, strong emotional reaction to something, it's because those reactions were first learned by us when our parents reacted to US that way when we were kids. Oftentimes, when they reacted poorly, it was because they were up against a personal limitation in their emotional resilience and competence.

(By the way, trying to improve upon the way we were parented as children does NOT mean that we don't love our own parents, or that we're blaming them or denigrating them. It really just means that we are trying to learn from the past and that we are trying to make things better for our own kids. But if we refuse to take a look at these things with an eye towards making them better, then we're at risk of passing along these reactions, fears, doubts, frustrations, etc., down to our own children.)

Some time ago I made up a term called Emotional Credibility which I defined as Trust + Likability. When we react immediately with a knee-jerk reaction because of some strong emotion, unless it's a true emergency, we generally lose some of our Emotional Credibility with the other person. This not only holds true with our kids, but with our spouses as well. That means that, unless there's some sort of emergency, reacting to our first-line, raw emotion tends to ultimately create a decrease in how much we are trusted, and therefore liked, by those around us.

On the other hand, when we try to approach our kids not reactively, but with a spirit of listening and seeking to truly understand their anger, frustration, confusion, disobedience, "laziness", etc., BEFORE reacting, only then are we well on our way towards building Emotional Credibility with them.

"SALLY-MARSHA-ANN-REILLY! YOU GET OVER HERE RIGHT THIS INSTANT!!!"

Have you ever heard yourself say something along these lines to your own child when you were angry? Where do you think you might have learned to do that?

Chances are, if you've done the above, your mother or father used your FULL name when they were angry. Does this have to be the case? No. But is it likely the case that you got it from them having done it to you? Yes, it is.

By the way, this "technique" makes for great dramatic flair and repetition of your own childhood past, but it does not make for very good connection or communication with your kids. In addition, it's not that effective a technique over the long haul either; the dramatic effect eventually sort of wears off and we're stuck only with the drama. What's more, we're teaching them that this is the way to handle themselves when they are angry with their own kids as well as how to address those kids (i.e., your grandkids).

Not a very good bag of tricks to pass along, I don't think.

Instead, try this:

"Sally, I've called you over here twice now. This is the last time before I come over to YOU. And if I have to do that they'll be consequences."

Much better. Now you've expressed to the child the situation, you've communicated where you stand, AND you've given them a choice. What you haven't done is snapped at them and bullied them into complying with you.

One way to summarize the above is that we as parents must work on earning our children's respect, not engendering their fear. We are always trying to build up the Emotional Credibility in our relationships with them, which will help make them strong and give us great satisfaction in the long run instead of frustration and guilt.

In other words, let's be our children's leaders and guides, not their bullies. Let's seek to understand, not to assume. And let's not train them to be somebody's victim when they grow up, neither emotionally nor physically.

We have to work on our knee-jerk, inherited reactions so that our kids are not stuck referring to them and acting them out once they grow up and become parents themselves. In other words, let's not pass that stuff down to them; instead, let's neutralize it and stop the cycle.

Incidentally, it's okay to have some doubts about your childhood and how you were raised. Some people worry that if they view this topic with a healthy, critical eye, it means that they don't love their parents. Nothing can be further from the truth. In my opinion, we honor our parents and our family lineage and legacy even more when we seek to preserve what was of value and to change what was hurtful or even threatening to our families' ability to thrive and to fly confidently in this world as time and the generations go by.

It's what I want my kids to do. I won't be offended. I'll be proud of them.

CHAPTER 48

LOSING YOUR HAPPY (Y)

You need a certain amount of peaceful emotional space in your life in order to grow and to live deliberately; otherwise, you may be surviving, but you're probably not thriving. I call this emotional space we all need our 'happy'.

After a while without our happy, we inevitably feel burnt out, more anxious, more hopeless and discouraged, less energetic and creative, less patient and empathetic, and, most importantly, less enthusiastic about our lives.

So what's the feeling one gets when one still has their happy? It's the feeling that life is good. You don't feel particularly rushed or stressed, and you're not full of anticipatory anxiety about tomorrow all the time. Doom and gloom is replaced with optimism and confidence; self-loathing and self-doubt with self-respect and self-assurance.

When you have your happy, you feel tranquil, at peace; you are not overly rushed and frenetic, and you feel a sense of mastery over your day and even your life. You are in an ideal state of mind and spirit in which to grow as a person and in which to live deliberately and more consciously. When you have your happy, you conduct yourself in relationships with less self-centeredness and with more empathy and understanding.

Now that you know what your happy is, I want to share with you some ways to get it back if you've lost it. The good news is that we seldom lose our happy permanently, and there's usually a way to get it back if we're willing to try.

The first way to begin working on getting your happy back is to make sure you've always got some flex time in your schedule. Chronically feeling like you're overworked and in a race with the clock is a sure way to eventually lose your happy.

If your week is so packed that you can't have much flex time, try to be sure to at least leave your weekends as free as possible for some regenerative rest and spontaneity. For example, I have resigned from certain professional organizations, groups, clubs, and other activities because, as much as I may have enjoyed them, they took up too much of my flex time and therefore threatened my happy. This has sometimes required some tough decision making, but I've always almost immediately felt the benefit, including having more time available to hang out with my kids which I enjoy and which helps me feel regenerated.

The second way to work on getting your happy back is to not chronically procrastinate. This one bad habit alone (i.e. procrastination) will produce so much subconscious guilt and anxiety in you that you'll have no chance at getting your happy back: you'll be too busy feeling guilty and vaguely anxious all the time. If you want to get your happy back, quit the habit of procrastination.

Thirdly, and closely related to the above: Take care of business. In other words, set up some kind of system or schedule that helps you get the necessities of your life done when they need to be done. There's nothing more toxic to your happy than not feeling like you have some degree of day-to-day mastery over your life.

Let yourself be proud of doing what you have to do and the quality with which you do it. (Don't strive for perfection, which can be crippling and work against getting your happy back.)

Once you've gotten your necessary tasks and obligations taken care of (taking care of business), and once you've both eliminated putting things off (procrastination) and stopped over-scheduling yourself (flex time), you will have the necessary emotional space and tranquility to relax and enjoy your life. Welcome your happy back!

By following steps one through three above you've eliminated some of the most common reasons why people lose their happy. Now you have no reason not to relax and enjoy your life a bit.

Oh, and for extra credit, you should also learn the serenity prayer, which asks for the serenity to accept what we cannot change, the courage to change what we can, and the wisdom to know the difference between the two. This is an absolute necessity and it will round out your program very nicely.

CHAPTER 49

WHY IT'S IMPORTANT TO LVAC WITH YOUR CHILD (K)

LVAC stands for: Listen, Validate, Ask, Comment. Most people pronounce it "L-VAC".

I invented and developed LVAC with a sole purpose in mind: to remind us how to give each other what we need most when communicating with one another.

It is especially important to LVAC with your children for three reasons:

1) it builds up your Emotional Credibility with them (a term meaning trust + likability)

2) it helps them learn more about themselves while you are learning about them at the same time

and

3) they'll never outgrow the need for it since we all need it

For example, if your child came to you and told you that they lost the locket or keychain you gave them for their birthday, or if they came to you and told you they had just been bullied at school or at the park? What would you do first?

What would you do if your child told you they were scared, worried, or angry about something?

What do you do when your child "talks back" to you?

Most of us, given the above situations, will make some sort of immediate comment to the child. We'll usually make some sort of generalization, or ultimatum, or maybe get defensive somehow.

What we tend NOT to do is to take the approach I'm about to outline for you. It's called the LVAC approach or technique, and it's explained more fully elsewhere in this book.

LVAC stands for Listen, Validate, Ask, and Comment and it goes like this: Rather than Comment immediately, first Listen to what they are saying, then Validate their feelings on the matter (e.g. "I see", "Oh, I can understand that", "Uh-huh, I see", "Yeah?", etc.). Then, once we've listened and validated, we can then move on to Asking some questions. The best questions to ask are open-ended questions, such as "How'd you feel about that?", or, "Then what?"

The use of open-ended questions with your child will help them clarify what they are trying to say to you, and, perhaps more importantly, to themselves. A great deal of the magic of the LVAC technique lies within the Asking of open-ended questions step, as we resist the temptation of making immediate Comments. A good open-ended question encourages the other person to talk more rather than shutting down.

Don't make the mistake of using closed-ended questions such as, "You're not wearing that are you?", or, "I hope you didn't do that, did you?" These are actually just Comments in disguise. The problem with Commenting as a first response is that the Comment tells the child about where WE are emotionally, it does not help us learn about THEM, and it does not help them learn about themselves.

Perhaps one of the most serious concerns about starting out with Commenting is that it short-circuits the process of allowing the child to learn about how they truly feel, so that they can learn to communicate with words. The other option is for them to learn only how WE feel and to "act out" their own feelings that they don't know about, often with self-sabotaging behaviors that hold them back in life.

This last bit I just mentioned comes about because through our Commenting and lack of Listening and Validating, we are teaching them to be more in tune with us than with themselves. This is also how parents pass their life traumas, worries, and limitations onto their children, generation after generation; through their Comments. Finally, going about it this way (i.e. Comments first) will not gain us any Emotional Credibility with them, since they will begin to realize over the years, at some level or another, that we always make it about ourselves instead of about them, forcing them to eventually pull away from us and to no longer trust us enough to come to us when they need us most.

Another problem with starting off with Comments is that it promotes DISCONNECT, not connection, between parent and child, as well as between them and themselves. These disconnects are what ultimately lead to destructive acting out behaviors both in childhood and in adulthood.

In summary, the LVAC technique will help you behave in a calm, focused, productive, and invaluable manner with your child so that they will get from you an important part of what they need from you as your child because, in addition to all the other important things we do for them in their lives, they need us as sounding boards and not as continuous Commentators.

If we use LVAC, our children will learn important things about themselves, their hearts, and their minds. They will also learn that they can trust us with their hearts and minds, and they will grow to trust us and to want us around them for years to come because of this manner in which we've always approached them. And, most importantly, they will grow to know, to like, and to accept themselves as they become the strong, confident, and emotionally competent adults we want them to be.

.

CHAPTER 50

KEEPING YOUR CORE... WHILE MAKING AN IMPACT (Y)

As you progress through life and take on more responsibilities it becomes ever more important to have a personal core which defines the key aspects of who you are as a person; i.e., your beliefs, what you like and don't like, what you wish for and don't wish for, your interpersonal style, your overall ability to handle frustration and difficulty, and your capacity for stopping to relax or to reflect.

Without this personal core, we may be alright living our lives for a while, but we are at an increased risk of eventually experiencing some sort of 'midlife crisis' or some other kind of emotional cataclysm that might even involve self-sabotaging and destructive behaviors; 'acting out' behaviors that our subconscious minds produce as the temporary solution to the problem of having no true core.

If we happen to have people or organizations relying on us, it becomes even more dangerous to go along 'coreless' as we find ourselves faced with greater and more complex decisions the further along we go. Examples of this include the following: politicians who paint themselves into ideological corners based upon what they think the public wants to hear and will vote for rather than what they themselves truly believe, sports figures who try to be role models for kids but who have yet to become emotionally competent adults themselves, entertainers who are pressured to get high ratings or ticket sales no matter what the cost to their integrity, and parents who want to just be 'friends' with their kids while trying to bypass their adult role as teacher and guide for them.

In each of these examples, a trade-off is made: temporary gains made by sacrificing core values or core identity. The lesson is that people are made less effective and sometimes downright destructive the weaker and more nonexistent their core. I don't think that we as a society do a particularly good job of identifying a personal core for ourselves, nor do I think that we do a good job of teaching our children how do it.

In fact, I think that just the opposite is true: the more interconnected we become and as the internet and the media become one with each other and with us, the more we will learn to pay more attention to following trends and less to what's actually happening inside of us. Tomorrow's leaders and overachievers will continue to evolve in the direction of learning how to study specifically for and to perform very well on standardized tests, and of creating heuristics out of their educations; they may very well come out of their eventual Ivy League alma maters almost entirely ignorant of who they really are as people and without much introspection at all, and truly vulnerable to any and all outside pressures and expectations at the expense of having any semblance of a personal core to guide them.

As a result of the above trend, generalized anxiety is on the rise, as is divorce, as well as a general disconnect between people, including within families. At one's personal core is the fundamental ability, identified long ago by Freud, to work and to love. I have also added four other central characteristics to a personal core or true self: what one truly likes, doesn't like, wants, and doesn't want.

I believe that we need to do more than just live in continual reactivity to what is outside of ourselves; we also need to use life to learn about ourselves based upon our work lives and our relationships, as well as our likes, dislikes, what we want, and what we don't want. We need to keep in mind that there is an actual person inside of us and a process of self-discovery that's supposed to be going on. We're supposed to be learning more about that person as we observe our reactions to people, to ideas, to our work, and to our relationships, among other things. And we should be noting these observations as we go along, ever-honing our personal core.

CHAPTER 51

WHAT IS THE STORY YOU TELL YOURSELF ABOUT YOUR KIDS? (K)

The reason I ask this question is because the answer holds the key to understanding one of the fundamental reasons why we can automatically react negatively or inappropriately to our children the way we sometimes do. The answer to this question also gives us one of the key reasons why they can immediately push our buttons the way they do.

In my work, I have come to learn that we humans tell ourselves, often subconsciously, a 'story' about our kids. These stories, if we have an opportunity to uncover them and become aware of them, can, at times, be quite shocking and even completely unacceptable to us, which is why they're often repressed into the subconscious to begin with. But it is nonetheless important that we uncover them and harvest them in order to ultimately defuse them of the enormous power that they have over us and how we react to and treat our kids.

For example, you might, for some inexplicable reason, see little Tommy as a future petty thief or criminal who will have no chance at a normal, productive life in society. In other words, the story you tell yourself about Tommy influences you by making you look down upon him and treat him negatively, whether you know about the story consciously or not.

Maybe you see little Sally as a weak little creature who will grow into an abused, unhappy, and self-loathing victim who ultimately takes her own life. Or perhaps the story goes that she will never make it in the harsh, cruel world; she just doesn't have the survival skills or the guts for it and she will fail.

Maybe little Jimmy will never be a "real man" when he grows up. Maybe your story says that he'll always be somewhat wimpy, effeminate, or "casper-milk-toast" and that he'll never have a relationship or be able to work and help support a family.

It could be that your subconscious story about little Wendy involves her ultimately abandoning you or betraying you somehow; that all your love and work will go unthanked and taken for granted.

Whatever the story, it's important that you become consciously aware of it, no matter how painful it might be to acknowledge, because the stories we tell ourselves about our children influence the way we deal with them. And what fuels these stories is often not consciously known to us, though possibilities include that the child reminds us of ourselves (identification), or perhaps of a parent or some other person from our own life story (transference).

The main point is that if my subconscious story about my child is that they will never make it in the world, for example, or that they have some sort of major disadvantage in life or character flaw, I may unknowingly project those subconscious fears and beliefs onto the child, which can fundamentally change their emotional development, including the formation of their self-esteem.

Rest assured that these fears most definitely did not begin in the child, but also know that we can and do project them onto the child; that is, if the fears are in the subconscious and unknown to us, we are at risk of acting on them, (thus the term "acting out"). On the other hand, if we bring our story into the conscious realm where we can know about it, we will at least have a chance of not acting it out, i.e., of not having the story dictate how we interact with the child.

I have seen many instances in which a parent could not explain their behaviors or attitudes towards their child until they began to learn more about their subconscious story regarding that child. You see, the whole point of the subconscious is to protect us from thoughts or feelings that our conscious minds deem unacceptable to us. Things like murderous feelings, sexual fantasies, rage, and jealousy, are often too hurtful for us to know about consciously and to admit to, so our bodies repress them into the subconscious realm where we might only catch small glimpses of them in our convoluted nightmares or "Freudian slips".

Isn't it frightening to think that, as much as we love our kids and would do anything for them, we also harbor subconscious stories about them which can ultimately harm them through our behaviors towards them and our reactions to them; behaviors and reactions which may very well help make these stories come to fruition?

In fact, these stories can influence the entire tenor of our relationship with our kids. So, if my subconscious story about little Tommy is that he's a manipulative little sociopath, guess what I'll treat him like? Or if I habitually interact with little Sally like she's a hopeless casualty of her own life, guess what

I'll ultimately and inadvertently be helping her prepare to become?

My suggestion would be to try to find a way, whether by writing about it, talking about it, or by whatever other method might work best for you, to uncover your subconscious stories about your kids. That way, you will be able to tell how much of any particular story is appropriate or fitting for whom a particular child actually is, rather than simply acting on what the story says about them. You will likely be surprised (and relieved!) by the differences that you find.

The bottom line is that we must strive to learn more about who our children really are, rather than what we might project onto them. We must get to know them without assuming that we already do. We can use tools like LVAC, which is found elsewhere in this book, and which reminds us to ask them questions and to let them talk to us and define themselves to both us and to themselves.

If, for example, while uncovering your story about them it turns out that they remind you too much of yourself or of someone you know, and if that's not a good thing to you, then try to focus on aspects of them that do NOT remind you of these people. Try to remember that they are a blank slate with some of your genetics attached, but that's about it. They don't have the life experiences (and traumas) which complete whom WE ended up becoming, which is different from who THEY are right now.

We must help our children to grow into who they truly are, not who we tell ourselves they are, so that we'll be able to enjoy them more and feel less guilty and upset about our day-to-day interactions with them.

CHAPTER 52

LISTENING BUILDS HOPE (Y)

Have you ever wondered why you are drawn to certain people in your life in an overwhelmingly positive way? Is it their charisma? Is it their charm or their intelligence? Perhaps it's the way they make you feel? I would say that, for me, it has most often been that I am drawn to people who project hope in some way or another.

Let me explain.

Books and articles on leadership, psychology, motivational speaking, teaching, and sales, among other fields, often expound upon the importance of how we leave each other feeling after we interact with one another; and there are frequently diverse agendas in this type of literature, either spoken or unspoken, behind wanting to make people feel a certain way—whether that be to teach, to sell, or to motivate and lead.

How about wanting to give hope in a different way and for a different purpose; with a different intentionality, so to speak?

I know two things about hope: the first is that when people receive hope, it has a healing effect on them. It helps activate in them their finest courage, their most boundless energy, and their greatest creativity. It feeds them and it sustains them.

People get stronger with hope. The second thing I know is that the giver of hope also receives these very same gifts.

Regarding my first observation about hope, most of us can remember at least one or two people in our respective childhoods who made us feel good about ourselves and who gave us hope; they helped us feel inflated, more centered, more secure, and stronger. We felt more loved AND more loving around them. As for the second observation, those of us who are now parents or are otherwise caregivers can almost certainly recall times when we've felt sustained and immensely satisfied by giving selflessly to our children or the others we've cared for; by giving them hope.

Both giver and recipient benefit when hope is given. And we can give hope naturally and elegantly every day by following a few simple steps:

First, Listen.

Listening is a true discipline that not only requires daily practice, but that also causes a deep and profound rewiring in us as we practice it. By teaching ourselves to habitually gear our topmost energies towards Listening rather than Commenting, whether we are at home with our families or out in the world, we will be on our way to helping others feel more hopeful by providing them with our receptive intentionality. First, we receive them, whatever they bring to us and even if we don't immediately agree with them.

At the same time, this rewiring towards Listening first helps us as well.

Why? Because an awful lot of the Comments we make to our spouses, to our children, to our colleagues, and to our coworkers are ultimately expressions of or our own insecurities, triggers, and anxieties, and, depending on the specific Comment, perhaps even our lack of hope. Think about it: Most of the time when we speak, unless we are teaching something very specific such as a language, we are speaking because of a series of internal emotional reactions which have ultimately led to the moment of needing to speak, i.e, of making a Comment.

Speaking of reactions, Commenting is most often a form of reacting. In other words, it's ultimately about us, not really the other person, and other people can sense this.

On the other hand, when we Listen, we are gearing our energies in the direction of the other person—and this transmits and projects hope.

When I'm with someone who is filled with anxiety, worry, or self-doubt; first, I Listen.

When I'm with someone who seems eager to argue; first, I Listen.

When I don't know what to say or how to help or what someone wants from me; first, I Listen.

Listening gives hope, and it often does so without a word.

It is the intention of Listening, which is communicated subconsciously, that does the healing; the intention of always starting with the practice of Listening rather than Commenting.

In closing, I'll share with you a mnemonic I made up some years ago to help me remind myself of what we've been discussing. It's called LVAC and it goes like this:

L.V.A.C. (pronounced "elvak")=Listen first, then Validate feelings, then Ask open-ended questions, then Comment, if necessary.

The key is to follow the first step always, and the rest when you can and with the best effort you can muster.

We all have the power to help others heal by giving them hope within the shadow of our passing presence in their lives, however brief or long it might be.

You can read all about the healing effects of LVAC elsewhere in this book. Do it now while the iron is hot!

CHAPTER 53

WILL YOUR KIDS VISIT YOU IN THE NURSING HOME? (K)

Will your kids visit you in the nursing home?

No doubt a somewhat brutal question, but I nonetheless use

this question in my practice precisely because it is such a hard one to ignore, and because it paints a strong, unforgettable image in our minds and in our hearts. This rather morbid question also serves as a way of asking ourselves if we've got enough Emotional Credibility with our kids, where Emotional Credibility = trust + they like us and want to be around us. Considering the above question, if you do, they'll visit you; if you don't, they won't.

Ok, let's continue with a few more questions: How do you talk to your kids? Are you respectful? What is your tone?

Sometimes a parent will tell me that their kids do not respect them, yet, from the way they describe it, they do not behave respectfully towards their kids either. "Yeah, but they're the one who have to respect us!", they tell me. Well, yes and no.

I want to clarify two things: First, one of our jobs as parents, other than to love our children unconditionally, is to TEACH. The other job is to LEAD; not to make constant ultimatums or threats, and not to throw tantrums ourselves. We are not doing it right if we find ourselves constantly nagging them, yelling at them, or making continuous comments or threats at them.

The jobs are to teach and to lead. If I do not treat my kids with respect and with proper leadership, whether that be with the tone that I use or in the way I behave towards them, under what sky in this universe should I expect that they will truly respect me? (By the way, I'm talking about respect here, not pure terror masquerading as respect.)

Respect begets respect. If I treat you with respect, then you will tend to be more respectful towards me. If I do not, neither will you.

It is especially important to teach respect by leading with respect. Friends and family who have served in the military tell me that they would have been willing to follow a leader that they respected and trusted into highly dangerous and risky situations if they had to do so. This was a person who led by example, by being ready to do themselves what he or she asked others to do; someone who led by teaching and guiding.

Our kids are watching us. They are observing how we lead. Young children don't yet have the distractions and responsibilities of adulthood like rent or a mortgage, and they don't yet have spouses and kids of their own; therefore they are focused on observing us, and they are doing it when we least realize it.

They are listening to our tone. They are observing our behavior. And, perhaps most importantly, they are, on some level, continuously tabulating an assessment of who and what we are; an indicator which I call Emotional Credibility, defined as the degree of trust we have in someone, and, therefore, how much (or how little) we want them around us.

In the end, as the years go by with our kids, we will either have passed or failed them on a very basic, fundamental, subconscious level; in other words they will ultimately either trust us and want to be around us, or they won't. To get back to the original question, they're either going to visit, or they're not.

They are observing us and asking:

What's this guy's limit?

How does she handle herself when she's overwhelmed?

Can I trust him with emotionally loaded subjects, or can I trust him with my emotions at all?

Should I generally avoid engaging her?

Will he shame me, reject me, or otherwise make me feel badly about myself?

Does she seem to genuinely like me and enjoy me, or do I always feel like a burden or a job to her?

Is he always distracted or multitasking around me, or does he actually stop, focus, and pay real attention to me for a couple of minutes?

Is she always angry?

Does he always say he's too tired to play?

Does she seem jealous or seriously upset when I win?

The list goes on and on....

Over the years, I've heard many people tell me how "it's been awhile" since they've visited their elderly parents, whether literally in a nursing home, or otherwise.

"Oh, we've really been pressed for time lately", they might say, or, "I've really just been too busy and exhausted to visit". Translation, according to the theory in this chapter: "My parent long ago burned through any Emotional Credibility (trust + my wanting to be around them) that I had in them, so I've really got no true attachment to them anymore other than one based on guilt and obligation. I've got very little, if any, true, positive and joyful, loving feelings for them that make me WANT to be around them; only feelings of guilt and obligation about visiting them."

This is one of the saddest things that I hear on a regular basis in my office.

Another variant of this is that the person does visit them or talk to them on the phone regularly, but only out of guilt and not out of the joy and love and "like" which comes from having great Emotional Credibility with someone.

Guilt and obligation are not what we're aiming for here. The real question is, will our kids visit us because we've earned it? Will they WANT to be around us? In order for this to happen, we have to earn our children's love and respect by working on building Emotional Credibility with them.

Any parent who still believes that "they should respect me just because I'm their parent" is unfortunately investing in fool's gold. The truth of the matter is that they might look like they respect you, but what they tell me when they're all grown up is that they actually feared you or dreaded you, or perhaps even pitied you. Not what we want.

I don't know about you, but I for one do not want my kids visiting me in the nursing home or calling me on the phone because they have feelings of guilt or obligation borne of fear, dread, or pity. No, I want my kids to actually trust me with their hearts, to see me as a loving leader.

I want them to enjoy me and to know that, ultimately, I enjoy them as well. I want to talk to them with respect, in a tone which conveys leadership and guidance, and with a spirit which treats them like the future adults (parents, husbands, wives, etc.) that they will someday become.

Otherwise, someday, we might identify very strongly with the words in Harry Chapin's song:

"I've long since retired, my son's moved away

I called him up just the other day

I said, 'I'd like to see you if you don't mind'

He said, 'I'd love to, Dad, if I can find the time

You see my new job's a hassle and the kids have the flu

But it's sure nice talking to you, Dad

It's been sure nice talking to you'"
("Cat's in the Cradle" by Harry Chapin, 1974 album Verities &
Balderdash)

CHAPTER 54

THE LONG GOODBYE: HOW THE ACKNOWLEDGEMENT OF DEATH CAN HELP
US REALLY LIVE (Y)

No, I'm not referring to the 1953 novel by Raymond Chandler, nor the 1973 film adaptation of the same by Robert Altman. What I'm talking about here is that feeling you get when you reach a certain age, say somewhere in your 40s or 50s, that one day you won't be around anymore and that you'll leave behind all the people, places, and things you love so dearly.

Heavy stuff. One of the things that helps make it easier to keep perspective each day; something that helps me behave in a more deliberate and Emotionally Competent manner on a day to day basis is the sobering thought that one day I won't be around anymore.

I try to let this reality influence my behaviors and choices each day, because I believe that we tend to behave better and more deliberately when we know that there is a time limit to life. I am consistently and regularly touched by this fact. Yes, it's a sad thought, but the truth and soberness of it can really help us to feel more appreciative and thankful on a daily basis and can help create more authentic moments of joy and healing.

For example, this thought will sometimes occur to me when I'm about to react badly to my kids or my wife; or to a neighbor, a friend, a sibling, or to a particular situation. It'll sometimes occur to me when I'm alone and obsessing about whatever stressful issues or challenges I am facing at that particular time:

'My life is not infinite. One day I'll be gone. This moment counts and is real so let me do my best right now to have more patience, more kindness, and more willingness to listen and learn before I react.'

So many of the traumas people have experienced in their early lives involve interactions they've had or things that have happened to them which were a direct result of someone not behaving in an Emotionally Competent manner with them. Whether they were punished too often or unfairly, discouraged from being who they truly were, neglected, steamrolled, or bullied by their parents, teachers, or coaches, or whether they were abused emotionally, physically, or sexually; whatever the case may be, things could have been different had the adults around them behaved in ways that reflected their knowledge of their own ultimate mortality.

We tend to behave better and more deliberately when we know that there is a limit to our lives. Life is real. The time limit is real: We're born. We go through childhood and schooling, striving to become independent and competent. We perform our life's work, whatever that may be. Maybe we build a family of our own. Then, as we get older and more frail, we eventually give up some or all of our hard-won autonomy and become dependent again. And, at some point, we die.

Life doesn't mess around. It's consistent in this every time; some version of the above scenario will happen to all of us, so what are we waiting for?

The next time your child comes to you when you're beside yourself with exhaustion and your patience has long ago been used up, think about the above fact. The next time your spouse needs some understanding or compassion (or mercy) from you, think about it then too.

The next time you find yourself caught up in feeling disrespected, insulted, or treated unfairly or when you've 'finally had enough', think about it then. The next time your parents or grandparents need you or you feel like they're a pain-in-the-you-know-what, think about it then too. And the next time you're all alone and you're feeling out of sorts, anxious, or fearful for no particular reason, think about it then.

Another way of saying all this is that nothing is permanent in life; it all goes away eventually. In fact, someone once told me that the way they dealt with school performance anxiety as a young adult was to ask themselves the question, "Will this grade count when I'm on my deathbed?" Not much will, so take it easy on yourself, and on others.

In other words:

Have more mercy.

Have more compassion.

Listen more.

Learn to let more go.

Comment less.

Ask more questions so you can learn more about what people are really trying to say to you.

Learn more and explore more and judge less.

Take care of yourself, but don't be too obsessive. The goal is to have quality of life, not to be a prisoner of perfectionism.

In sum, it is healthy to live our lives with the conscious, deliberate, working knowledge and acceptance that we do eventually die. This way, for example, when we look at our kids, they will see our true love shine through instead of chronic worry, anger, or exasperation. We will be more focused on them and less distracted by our neuroses. When we speak to our spouses, our tone will reflect our sincerest appreciation for them in our lives and our knowledge of their vulnerabilities and problems, as well as the things that we may be doing or saying to them that may be retraumatizing to them.

Singer Frank Sinatra sang about regrets and having 'too few to mention'. The surest way for us to be able to say the same thing is to deliberately live our lives each and every day; to interact mindfully with our loved ones and with others, focusing on our relationships and our passions instead of on acting out, in part because we consciously acknowledge and accept our mortality.

They say that if you need something done, give it to a busy person. In that spirit, if you want to live your best life here on Earth, live it knowing that there is a finite limit to it and then pour everything you've got into the time that you have.

Chapter 55

Not Acting Like a Victim (Y)

If you've ever heard someone say, "Stop acting like a victim", either to you or to someone else, what image comes to mind? Perhaps you've pictured someone who is being sort of whiny or complaining, or maybe passive or indecisive to the point of self-sabotage.

In this chapter, I want to tell you about a completely different variation on the theme of 'victimhood' than the above, one that will likely surprise you because it may not at all be what you're picturing. It is also more common than you might initially think.

Acting like a victim in the way I'm describing here involves four elements, each of which feeds off of the others:

1) it's blaming others instead of taking personal responsibility

2) it's chronic anger and negativity

3) it's being defensive

4) it's ugly

Acting like a victim, the way it's being described here, is 'ugly' because it drives people away from us. It makes us repulsive, so to speak, to others and not someone who they want to be around. As well, when someone is chronically angry, always defensive, and constantly blaming others, it doesn't take much imagination for us to see why folks wouldn't want to be around them.

Acting like a victim is 'defensive' because when we're acting like victims we take everything to heart as if it were a criticism and we get defensive about it. We are unable or unwilling to try to see if there is any truth to whatever is being said, or, at the very least, to just let it go. And with our defensiveness comes anger and blaming.

Also from the above list, acting like a victim is being chronically angry and negative about everything. When we're constantly feeling that the world is unfair to us or that everyone has it in for us, we remain chronically angry. When we are convinced that every circumstance has a reason why it won't work out well for us in the end and that every person is an enemy in disguise, we remain chronically angry.

The word unfair becomes our battle cry. When we can't stop and be satisfied or happy or at peace for even few minutes at a time. We are always waiting for the 'other shoe to drop' and we are never at ease or light of heart or relaxed, even for a little while.

Finally, when we habitually find ourselves blaming others for what they are making us feel or for what they are making us do, we are again acting like victims.

The problem with carrying ourselves through our lives as victims is twofold: firstly, we push others away and hurt them, and secondly, we can begin to dislike ourselves and to treat ourselves badly.

So, getting back to the original point, acting like a victim is not necessarily a passive, whiny, sort of stance or attitude like we might have assumed. On the contrary, when we're acting like victims we can also be quite overtly offensive, and we can often stir up anger, fear, anxiety, confusion, and resentment in those around us, including our loved ones.

So now that we've defined the problem, how do we fix it?

Here are three simple rules to follow in order to quickly 'pull the plug' on victimhood in your life:

1) Accept responsibility for what you can control, and let go of the rest.

2) Don't blame or attack others.

3) Be kind to others and to yourself; you are not perfect and are not expected to be perfect.

Whenever you are tempted to be defensive, blame, or get angry again, try to step back, take a breath, and go through the above steps to determine where the problem is and how you can best correct it move on. By the way, having a sense of humor, both towards yourself and the situation at hand, even if it's a little forced, can be a boon in just about any situation, as can the mantra, "Let it go."

Most folks I've met who routinely act like victims are fundamentally good people who carry heavy loads in their lives; for some it's about past traumas, for others, mostly current situations. Yet others are dealing with both past and present issues that trigger victimhood in them.

Whatever the case may be, when we are acting like victims the way I'm describing it here, we are acting out our wounds and we are bleeding all over the place. That's literally what it looks like and feels like to those around us. They see it. They feel it. And it's toxic to them.

We must stop bleeding all over those around us, and we must put some salve on our wounds by learning to acknowledge their effects on us and by moving on from them today, at least with our outward behaviors. Then, we must do the same thing tomorrow.

CHAPTER 56

RAISING VICTIMS (K)

In my first book, Cobwebs and Ugly Wallpaper, I wrote a chapter called "Raising Victims" about the habits and behaviors we parents get into with our children, and, in particular, the ones that can breed adult tendencies towards victimhood. Some of the things we do include having poor boundaries with them, and angry, controlling behaviors which give us relief in the moment but which train them to be treated the same way by other people later on in their lives.

Right now, though, I want to look at a slightly different angle on raising victims. Specifically, I want to look not at how the child gets trained to being treated by others, but, instead, on the impact of childhood trauma on the later development of destructive habits and lifestyle choices which contribute to adult health problems, shortened longevity, and other self-care and quality of life issues. In other words, I want to look at how we ultimately become victims to ourselves.

If you've read any of my previous books or essays, you've read about the deleterious effects of emotional disconnects, especially the ones in childhood but also current ones in adulthood, on our eventual emotional health as well as the things (often unhealthy, self-destructive things) we do to try to feel reconnected or 'alive' again.

For example, a wife who doesn't feel emotionally connected to her husband and uses 'retail therapy' in order to fill in the emptiness that the disconnect creates.

Or a man who doesn't feel particularly connected to anybody in his life and uses pornography to fill in the emptiness.

The examples are many, and they include all of us in our own specific ways, both big and small: it's just a matter of finding the right set of circumstances and flavor of acting out behaviors for each of us. If we look at the very beginnings of disconnectedness in our lives, it usually starts in those earliest years of childhood when we're not feeling empathically connected to our original caregivers, usually the parents.

Of course, this general statement begs the question: What makes a child feel connected? Being Listened to. Being Validated. Being Asked some open-ended questions about what they are trying to tell us. And, importantly, saving our Comments or opinions for after we're done doing the first three things.

My LVAC® Technique puts this in mnemonic form so it's easy to remember. It stands for Listen, Validate, Ask, Comment, and it helps us to connect more and to disconnect less. LVAC works not only with children, but also with spouses, friends, acquaintances, and anyone else we happen to be having a conversation with.

Without the LVAC approach, there is great potential for disconnect, and, as you now know, where there is disconnect there is the likelihood of destructive behaviors that are used to fill the emptiness created by the same. This happens all the time, in all of us, no matter how subtle or how obvious. These habits and behaviors are often of momentary pleasure, but not what we actually wanted long-term, thus the term 'destructive'.

The most extreme forms of disconnect in childhood are created by frank abuse (emotional, physical, sexual) and severe neglect. There are many roads to these situations and they happen in all sorts of families, even the ones that look perfectly fine from the outside. In addition, and especially in cases other than the frank abuse or severe neglect ones, parents often don't even realize that they're setting their kids up for feelings of disconnect and emptiness later in life:

Johnny: "Dad, come here and check this out."

Dad: "Not right now Johnny, I'm busy."

Sound familiar?

Of course it does because we do it all the time! Not exactly frank abuse or neglect. However, a steady diet of "Not right now Johnny" or constant, reflexive renditions of "No!" without really listening or validating Johnny's desire, eventually start to add up to Johnny's lack of feeling connected to the parent. Disconnect slowly creeps in, and destructive behaviors eventually develop to fill in the emptiness we've helped create.

Or how about:

Sally: "I'm scared about what will happen in school tomorrow in math class."

Mom: "Well, you should have studied then, shouldn't you have?! Instead of spending all that time on your phone!"

Now, most of us would agree that mom is, in fact, correct here, but where's the empathy? And, yes, I do understand that maybe this was the billionth time Sally has done this, but we must still be careful about the temptation to constantly blame or Comment immediately (see LVAC above) without first showing some empathy and understanding. Without it, we again are left with disconnect.

The problem is, we care about our children so much that we impulsively Comment before we've truly Listened and Validated. We're too close to them, too concerned and tied into them, and rightfully so; after all they are our kids, and we love them. It's too hard to be calm and objective with them, and it shows. I often joke that I could probably be a better parent to the neighbors' kids than to my own. But, take heart, it's not any one particular episode that creates the disconnect between us and our kids, but the steady accumulation.

The greater the accumulated disconnect, the more emptiness they will feel, and the greater the chance that they will eventually develop habits and behaviors that will be destructive to their health, quality of life, and longevity; habits and behaviors which will give them momentary relief from the pain, numbness, and emptiness created by the disconnects within.

They will likely be unaware consciously of the disconnects within and, instead, they might think that the problem is simply boredom, frustration, or some sort of nebulous anxiety. The real problem is that they will use things like food, alcohol, drugs, sex, material goods, gambling, risk taking, or thrill seeking in order to temporarily feel better: Eventually come the weight issues, the cholesterol and type II diabetes problems, the liver and kidney issues, cancers of various kinds, heart attacks, strokes, and the list goes on and on, as the unhealthy habits and behaviors of adulthood become the tragic vestiges of our early childhood disconnects.

By now it should be obvious that there is a direct connection between destructive habits and behaviors that are meant to ease the pain and fill the emptiness of the disconnects within, and the eventual health problems, quality of life issues, and shortened lifespan that arise. So while it's valuable to examine the relationships between diet, lifestyle choices, substance abuse, stress, and our overall health, it's also vital to look at the emotional traumas and ensuing disconnects of childhood that play such a major role in laying the foundation of emotional pain which we eventually deal with by making unhealthy choices in these areas later on as adults.

Chapter 57

Settling Down (M)

As we go forward in our lives, at some point many of us ask the question, "Is this it?"

In fact, people often come to my office with this very question implicit in their presenting problems, but using other names for it such as 'marital problems', 'problems at work', 'anger problems', or even general anxiety and depression problems, without realizing that at the heart of their issue lies the unspoken and often unconscious question, "Is this it?"

Interestingly, the way we often express this question ends up being more through our behaviors than through actual recognition and verbalization; behaviors which are often destructive. (These would be the so called 'acting out behaviors' such as drinking too much or doing drugs, pornography and extramarital affairs, emotional neglect of the marriage or the children, inappropriate spending, self-sabotage at work, etc.)

The antidote to all of this aimlessness and angst is found in two somewhat etherial but potentially healing words: Settling Down. What do you think of when you think of those two words? Honestly. Do they frighten you or make you anxious? Do you think, "I'm settling!", or maybe, "I'm down!"

Notice how these two simple words can have such negative or threatening connotations. Some have even argued that a major reason for human pain and suffering, including many anxieties and fears, is an unconscious fear of death and mortality. The argument goes that we never settle down because that means the struggle is over and THAT must equate death, right?

There is even a school of existential therapy that begins work by first addressing this crippling, unconscious death anxiety and proceeds forward from that point, in the belief that once we get that dealt with, we can eventually settle down and live our lives consciously and deliberately rather than unconsciously and reactively.

Now the above may all be well and true, but what I'm presenting here is actually not that deep or profound. It is simply this: At some point, each of us needs to be reconciled within ourselves to certain assumptions about our lives, so that we can build the rest of our lives upon that foundation.

Let's take marriage for example.

I've come across so many couples who eventually fall out of love and get divorced that I actually wrote a book about it called, "Don't Get Married! Unless You Understand A Few Things First", in which I coin The 3 Plus One Rule. The Rule states that unless there is: 1) violence, 2) drugs and alcohol, or 3) habitual infidelity, or unless there is indifference and unwillingness to work on the marriage (the Plus One), that marriage is an 'innocent marriage'. (There's a bit more to it, but you can read more about it in my marriage book if you're interested.)

So, an innocent marriage is one that doesn't have any of the four factors I've just described, which means that in the case of an innocent marriage gone bad, a major part of the problem is often one of not settling down. In other words, one or both spouses have not yet truly decided to settle down with the other in the marriage. They're not all in. On some level, they're not fully committed to the marriage, whether they know it or not, and it's causing problems.

Picture a three legged race. Now, if the tie that binds your leg to your partner's is made of string, it will be much easier to break than if it were made of leather or chains. In the former situation, as the race progresses onto rough terrain, the partners may decide that it's just too hard to continue on with their legs tied together, and they may therefore decide to break the string. In the latter scenario, however, the one where the tie is made of either leather or chains, the partners are committed; that means they'll have to come up with a way to make it through the event together.

It's really just a matter of necessity being the mother of invention. That is, in being absolutely committed to one another via unbreakable bonds, they are quite literally forced to come up with different solutions and may even need to travel along entirely different pathways compared to the uncommitted partners who have the option of simply breaking off from one another.

The problem is that the couple who can easily break their bonds misses out on the opportunity to experience something new, something outside the realm of their prior experiences. They will never see nor feel what it would have been like to fully experience the event together, complete with new pathways and insights. Instead, they will merely repeat the old feelings and tired scenarios of the past.

Another way of saying all this is that the partners who committed to one another were forced to grow, both as a couple, and as individuals. And I would argue that the same idea holds true in other areas of life as well. We need to consciously and deliberately commit; to ourselves, to our spouses, to our children, to our communities, to our work, and to our avocations.

We need to settle down. Only then will we have established some important, fundamental givens or assumptions for ourselves upon which we can, because these things are truly settled, build a foundation or platform from which we can spring upwards and outwards, full force and with greater energy and enthusiasm, into our lives.

G.K. Chesterton, the late 19th/early 20th century British ex-journalist who wrote the Father Brown mysteries which later became the BBC television series of the same name, was certainly no psychiatrist or therapist by any stretch. In fact, he was an atheist-turned-Catholic who was once reported to have said that psychotherapy was like Catholic confession without the absolution. You don't have to be a Catholic or a believer of any kind to read what he said about settling down. (In fact, if you ever get the chance to read any Chesterton, his book 'Orthodoxy' would be a great place to start. I believe it will enrich your life and add to what I'm saying here about settling down.)

I, like Chesterton, have been taught by both observation and experience that without the purposeful and deliberate step of committing, we are at great risk of living our entire lives as free floating and overly intellectualizing children of our time, just as many have done before us. By not settling down on at least some things, we are in danger of remaining indiscriminate and uncommitted to all things; and it's only a matter of time before we are eventually haunted by the question, "Is this it?"

Paradoxically, on the other hand, commitment leads to freedom. In other words, if I spend all of my years running and searching, I'll never get to see or feel what happens when I put some roots down; when I put into place certain givens and build a life upon them as best I can.

We often say to our children, "Okay, let's settle down now", but it is much more difficult to tell the child within ourselves to do the same thing. In the end, we've got to start somewhere in order to truly begin.

Chapter 58

Seeking to Truly Understand (Y)

Have you ever thought about your general approach to the people, events, and world around you? How often do you find yourself taking the time to ask questions and to explore instead of snapping to judgment? In other words, how often do you approach life from the perspective of trying to truly learn and understand rather than assuming or judging?

On the flip side, do you notice the people in your life who really seem to want to understand where you're coming from? How do you feel about them? My guess is it's a positive feeling. I think that most of us are habitually tempted to assume, categorize, generalize, pigeon-hole, and otherwise quickly and expeditiously dispatch with what others are saying to us and, more generally, with the events in our lives as well.

Think about it for a moment. Can you remember the last time in your marriage that you and your spouse didn't just give each other a quick, one or two word answer or comment? How about the last time you asked each other a friendly question or two in order to learn more about what the other person was really meaning, feeling, or thinking?

"Honey, I'm a little worried about next week."

"Oh, don't worry, you'll be fine."

What do you notice about this little interchange? What is evident to me is that the first person said that they were worried, and the second person simply made a comment. Now there may be several reasons why they did that. For example, maybe they just needed to make their own anxiety go away by fixing the problem, using the comment to end the potentially uncomfortable discussion. Perhaps they sincerely felt that by saying, "don't worry, you'll be fine", they had actually helped the other person.

In the end, they probably meant well, but were simply unaware that there was something more they could do, something better. When we seek to truly understand people, events, and life in general, we must ask questions. This behavior, as opposed to commenting right away, is literally a paradigm shift for most of us.

Asking questions does several important things: Firstly, it engages the other person. Secondly, it allows and helps the other person to think through the issue at hand. And thirdly, it gives both you and the other person the satisfaction of feeling that more has been truly understood and shared between you than perhaps might have been in the past, which builds intimacy.

It is important to most of us that we feel understood, at least (and perhaps especially) by the people we care about and who care about us. Children, for example, often grow quite upset during those moments when they are feeling misunderstood by their parents or siblings. And when they are first born, it is literally vital to their very survival that they, and their needs, are understood by their caregivers.

When we grow up, we are still yearning to be understood, and, on a subconscious level, it can still feel vital. There is immense emotional importance in feeling understood by our loved ones even in adulthood, and a buildup of disconnect and resentment if we are not. When my spouse says something to me and I make a quick, summarizing, or concluding comment in response, I have not truly sought to understand her. The result over time is disconnect, followed by loss of emotional trust (read about Emotional Credibility elsewhere in this book), and, eventually, resentment.

Why resentment? Resentment because if someone, especially a loved one, expends the neuronal energies required to put their thoughts together and to transport those thoughts across their nervous system and out of their mouth as words, then we should at least make an effort to understand what motivated those thoughts to form, and, ultimately, those words to come out; doing so is both a sign of respect and a sign of caring, and it builds the kind of trust and emotional connection that we humans need.

Luckily, you can use my simple acronym to automatically get yourself into an exploratory or learning mode: it's called LVAC®, which stands for Listen, Validate, Ask, then Comment last, if at all. By using the LVAC technique, you will automatically switch into exploratory mode and bypass the natural human tendency to want to Comment first like the person did in the unfortunate example I gave above.

Children will often Comment first, and that's okay. Emotionally competent adults, on the other hand, really do need to learn to Listen, Validate, Ask, and save the Comments for last. In other words, we adults need to learn that we need to learn, not Comment; we need to seek to understand.

Someone once told me that good advice fulfills two criteria: first, it needs to be as timeless and as universal as possible, and, second, it needs to be simple and true. Using these two criteria, I want to give you this simple advice: Do not make it a habit to assume.

When a loved one, or anyone else, talks to you, don't automatically assume you know what they are talking about. Instead, take a moment to Listen to them and to Validate or affirm what they're saying to you even with just a simple head nod or an "uh-huh" to encourage them to keep talking to you and expressing themselves.

Then, by all means, go ahead and use your voice and your command of the language to Ask them some open-ended questions, ones that encourage further conversation and exploration. Seek to truly understand in order to be sure that you've given them a chance to express their heart to you; so that you each come away feeling closer to one another as well as better understood.

CHAPTER 59

THE SIDE-EFFECTS OF CHRONIC MULTITASKING (Y)

Are you a chronic multitasker? Can you take a phone call, organize your to-do list, keep an eye on your child, answer the front door, brew some tea, and put a sweater on, all at the same time? This can be a good thing sometimes, but it can also be bad for you and I'll explain why.

We live in a world where multitasking has become the new zen, being practiced everywhere from the classroom to the living room. In fact, it seems that if you don't learn to multitask and to do it well in today's ultracompetitive world, your chances of excelling or even just keeping up begin to fall exponentially starting as early as middle school.

For adults, multitasking is also a way of feeling that we've done it all; that we've succeeded in gaining a feeling of mastery or control over the day, the hour, or the moment. Nothing got missed or got by us.

But what are the downsides of all of this? As a physician, whenever I prescribe a medication for someone, I always give them my speech about the "risks, benefits, side effects, and alternatives" of that medication, especially the ones with higher potential side effects or risks for the patient.

So what are the risks of multitasking? The main one is the loss of being present and Deliberate (I've capitalized it for a reason) in the moment. In other words, we risk disconnecting from ourselves, losing ourselves.

I want you to try this exercise: The next time you find yourself running a bit ragged, running in overdrive per se and doing a million things at the same time, STOP. Then, I want you to pick and do ONE thing; just choose something and carry it out with your full concentration and presence, i.e. do it Deliberately. (In my REALADULTS acronym the letter "D" stands for Deliberate living and "S" stands for Stopping.)

Next, notice what you feel. When I do this exercise, which I do regularly to recalibrate my pace and check in with myself during the day, I am able to literally feel an internal shift and a realignment of sorts.

Realignment of what?

A realignment with myself.

When we constantly multitask and never "check in", we set in motion a pace that can eventually get away from us. We lose the Deliberateness of our day, and we lose the connection with ourselves. Paradoxically, the thing we do to feel like we are in control (i.e. multitasking), actually promotes a feeling of being out of control and no longer at the helm of neither ourselves nor our lives. When we constantly run on higher octane fuel like this, we also increase the cumulative stress and internal wear and tear on our minds and bodies without realizing it---the price we pay for the higher level of performance.

In fact, I would wager that if you could somehow measure your own pulse, blood pressure, and cortisol level (i.e. the stress hormone) while you were in the groove of multitasking versus when you were Deliberately focusing on one task at a time and staying connected with yourself in the moment, you'd be surprised at what you'd find.

So is it okay to use the powerful technique of multitasking when you really need to? Yes, but it's when that's the ONLY gear in the shift box that we can get into trouble as we face the law of diminishing returns and disconnect within ourselves.

CHAPTER 60

THE ONE MINUTE TRICK (Y)

In order to truly excel in life and learn how to 'go', we must first learn how to STOP.

REALADULTS is an acronym I came up with some years ago that contains the ten essential adult emotional competency skills which are as follows: (R)estraint, (E)ngagement, (A)nxiety modulation, (L)VAC, (A)nger modulation, (D)eliberate living, (U)nconditional positive regard, (L)iving with pain and failure, (T)hank you/I'm sorry & tone, and (S)topping.

I want to teach you a simple trick to help you master the adult skill of Stopping.

What I mean by stopping is not the same thing as stopping while glancing at the T.V. or the newspaper, and it's not the same as stopping while working on the computer or tablet device. It's also not the same thing as sitting there worrying, planning, figuring, etc. Most of all, I definitely don't mean stopping when you are really just simply waiting to get moving again.

No, I would like to teach you how to truly Stop; how to fully pause your life for just a moment and experience what that feels like. For most of us this is a struggle to do at first, indicating just how thoroughly we've been trained to just keep on chugging along in life without ever learning to truly be still even for just a moment. We have been trained to live a reactive life, not a deliberate one.

Ok, ready for the trick?

Take a watch or clock that has a seconds hand (yes, you can use a digital device if you don't have a watch), and simply watch the seconds hand tick around for one full rotation without doing anything else.

Sounds simple right?

Well, try it.

Not so simple is it? In fact, that minute may have felt like an eternity!

I've had people come up with some pretty creative ideas on how to cheat this technique. So no, you can't watch T.V. or listen to music while doing it; and you can't pop popcorn or watch water boil either.

The key to this trick is to learn to be still. Expect your body to rebel, to try to get up and go---but don't let it! Instead, let yourself feel any feelings that come up…then let them pass.

"And", you ask, "what do I do if I've toughed it out and made it through the one minute trick?"

Well, that's easy: repeat it.

When you'd just as soon do another minute as you would move on with your day, you're ready to quit. You've truly experienced Stopping. Congratulations and well done.

Now do it again tomorrow.

CHAPTER 61

LEARNING TO STOP (Y)

In life, most of us already know how to GO GO GO.

What we're not so good at is knowing how to STOP!

From our earliest childhood days most of us were guided or directed to do all of the things that needed to be done at home or that were assigned to us at school. We then proceeded through grade school, perhaps some sort of college, vocational, or graduate school, and then, finally, off into the workforce. So far, so good.

By now many of us are also married, some with children, and we have other obligations such as bills, various professional and social commitments, etcetera: Let the frenetic multitasking begin. We know how to do all this; we have been trained for it from the start.

That being said, ask yourself this question: Am I comfortable with being still? In other words, do I know how to Stop? (And this includes your thoughts as well.)

We really need to take a step back and reassess how we pace ourselves in our lives and how we conduct our days, realizing that there is an actual skill involved that we need to learn, a skill that I call Stopping. The Stopping skill is part of my REALADULTS acronym (it's the "S" in REALADULTS), which I designed to help us remember the ten most important emotional competency skills, and which I cover in more depth elsewhere in this book.

When the maestro does his job with the orchestra, he or she not only guides the musicians as to when and how to play the notes, but also when to Stop. We need to become better maestros of our days. In fact, the concept of Stopping is both a universal and elegant part of nature, which we observe in both the animal and plant kingdoms, as well as in weather systems, the seasons, in geological and anthropological history, and even in the microbial evolution of infectious diseases.

In all, we humans are some of the least skilled creatures when it comes to knowing how to pace ourselves, which, of course, includes knowing how to Stop. Often, our only way to feel in control of our lives is to keep on going, a coping mechanism which then gets passed down to our children, as it probably got passed down to us, so that they too grow up not knowing about or practicing the skill of Stopping.

The problem many of have with Stopping is that it makes us uncomfortable. When we Stop, our thoughts come back to us. The momentary cessation of activity creates a vacuum which is immediately filled with our conscious and subconscious conflicts: our anxieties, worries, fears, resentments, rage, despair, helplessness, shame, etc.

Our usual solution to this barrage of emotional pain is to keep going! But we need to know that there is value in Stopping long enough to feel some of this pain, namely, that we learn that our pain is ultimately limited in nature, and that the pain alone won't kill us or make our worst nightmares come true the way we fear it might.

Of course, what we do with that subconscious pain in order to avoid it (like never Stopping), can, in fact, do these very things to us by making us unknowingly act out those unknown feelings of pain in destructive ways. As long as we learn to Stop long enough to learn about and feel what we are constantly running away from, we might actually get a chance to experience real joy rather than destructive behaviors and misery.

In my first book, Cobwebs And Ugly Wallpaper, there is an essay called "Running and Searching". What I meant by this is that we humans are constantly looking for the next great thing: the next cure for life itself, the next novelty, the next stimulus, the next thrill, the next guru or shaman, or the next inspiration.

It's like that song from Huey Lewis And The News:

"I want a new drug
One that won't make me sick
One that won't make me crash my car
Or make me feel three feet thick

I want a new drug
One that won't hurt my head
One that won't make my mouth too dry
Or make my eyes too red

I want a new drug
One that won't go away
One that won't keep me up all night
One that won't make me sleep all day

I want a new drug
One that does what it should
One that won't make me feel too bad
One that won't make me feel too good"

There is no cure for life. Life is, in part, painful. Stopping lets us acknowledge what it is that we are feeling and what it is that we are running from or trying to run towards. All of that 'running and searching', which is what we do when we're not Stopping, uses up our already limited time and energy.

We need to teach ourselves how to be still for even a minute or two at a time: I like to use the seconds hand on my old watch to sit and Stop while it makes at least one full rotation as I remain still. Try it.

We also need to teach our children that it's okay to Stop and sit with their emotions as well. They too are under a constant barrage of external stimulation, including video games, computers, tablets, cell phones, television, and movies, among other things. How many of us actually sit with our kids and just hang out with them or converse with them in a non-agenda driven, open-ended way?

Most of our lives are run by those same demands and agendas which, while useful and necessary to provided a degree of structure and productivity to our lives, also help to perpetuate our total dependency upon those very same things to tell us how to feel and what to do next, and next after that, and next after that....

We lose OURSELVES.

Let's work on finding our way back to ourselves and let's also help our children not lose themselves in the first place.

In other words, let's learn how to Stop.

CHAPTER 62

REALADULTS (Y)

I came up with the acronym "REALADULTS" as a way to permanently give people the ten major adult skills we need in order to behave like emotionally competent, mature adults, despite childhood beginnings and traumas. My thought was that, once memorized, people could take the REALADULTS tool with them wherever they went, referring to it often and in any situation they came across in their lives. And, I figured, the more we practiced these ten essential skills, the better the results.

But before I tell you all about what each letter in REALADULTS means, let me just say that each of the ten skills in the acronym has been distilled from years of practice helping people overcome the adverse childhood circumstances which affected their personality development, and, therefore, the way that they behave. This includes all of us, since we each have a certain personality structure which was heavily influenced not only by genetics but by the events of our childhoods as well. The goal of REALADULTS, and what really motivated me to invent it, is to help people learn behaviors which they would have learned had childhood circumstances been optimal; i.e., it is designed to help us behave more like the person we'd have become without the trauma overlay on our personality structure.

Without further delay, let's take a look at REALADULTS.

REALADULTS stands for:

R=restraint
E=engagement
A=anxiety modulation
L=LVAC (see elsewhere in this book for the meaning of the adult skill LVAC)
A=anger modulation
D=deliberate living
U=unconditional positive regard
L=living with pain and failure
T=saying Thank you and I'm sorry (also Tone)
S=stopping

And now, a brief description of each of these skills. I won't go overly into detail for now, as I really just want you to get a general sense of each skill, just enough to go out and get started practicing them.

R=Restraint
This is a major adult skill, which is why I placed it in the first position of the acronym. How many people do you know that show restraint in their lives? How about yourself? Are you one to quickly react or respond right away, to immediately judge, try to fix, or make a comment? Or do you try to restrain your first impulse and see what happens when you hold back a moment and let things unfold a bit? This is especially important when interacting with children, when sometimes all that's needed is a little restraint before we unload on them or project shame or blame onto them that can affect their lives for a very long time. Lacking in restraint with your spouse can severely limit your Emotional Credibility with them, a term which I've defined elsewhere in this book as Trust+Likability, and, as a

result, can create resentment as well as both emotional and physical disconnect between you.

E=Engagement

By this I mean engagement in your life. How much mastery do you have over your life? Do you like your life or are you generally a person who feels overwhelmed or miserable a lot of the time? Engagement is when we are really plugged into our lives. It's the unleashing of our truest selves upon our lives, complete with joy, creativity, energy, commitment, and connectivity, among other things. If you spend a lot of your time feeling empty, bored, or disengaged, then it's time to explore ways to get engaged with your life!

A=Anxiety modulation

This means the ability to deal with, or modulate, anxiety. In order to get good at the adult skill of Restraint (above), we must work on our ability to manage anxiety. When people have minimal skill in modulating their anxiety, you can see it in the way they need to react right away; the need to have an immediate solution or "fix" to a problem. In other words, they are VERY uncomfortable with uncertainty, fear, lack of control, loose ends, etc. Not practicing the adult skill of anxiety modulation can lead to trouble in our relationships as well as in other parts of our lives.

L=LVAC

LVAC stands for Listen, Validate, Ask, Comment. It is a trademarked technique I came up with to remind us to Listen first, then Validate the person who is talking to us. Then, as appropriate, we should Ask them open-ended questions about what they are saying or feeling before we, at last and if at all, Comment. The problem is that we tend to Comment FIRST because of our lack of anxiety modulation skills (see above) and our need to judge, fix, or otherwise communicate our agenda to the other person instead of Listening first and seeking to truly learn about what the other person is trying to say. When we fail to do LVAC regularly with children, for example, we slowly, over time, replace their budding inner agendas and growing self-knowledge with our own anxiety-ridden ones. They eventually lose touch with themselves and, instead, learn all about OUR inner conflicts and anxieties. We essentially hamstring their development with our Comments and they grow up feeling empty, lonely, and disconnected from themselves, a recipe for disaster and eventual acting out behaviors in an attempt to fill the void inside.

A=Anger modulation
Same idea as the anxiety modulation skill, only this one involves anger. We often don't know how to handle the anger emotion very well. We often try to suppress it consciously, or repress it automatically without even knowing that we were angry, or we might overreact and blow up. Instead of any of these options, we need to learn how to deal with anger in healthy ways. For example, we are often afraid to talk about or show our anger because on some level we're trying to take care of other people's feelings and reactions at the expense of our own. This only makes matters worse and can help turn simple anger into rage (which I equate to the combination of anger + fear), or even depression (subconscious anger turned towards the self.)

D=Deliberate living

Simply put, living deliberately is the opposite of living reactively. You can therefore see how living deliberately would involve some of the other adult skills we've talked about so far, including anxiety modulation and restraint. Living deliberately, in a nutshell, means putting things into our lives that we want there and not putting things into our lives that we do not want there. So, if we are acting out by drinking, having affairs, or going on buying sprees, for example, we will eventually have to deal with the destructive results and consequences of those behaviors; things which we do not want in our lives. Living deliberately means choosing purposely and purposefully how we want to live out our lives.

U=Unconditional positive regard

Unconditional positive regard means benefit of the doubt. It is very different from unconditional love, which we can really only ever get from our parents (or God if you're a person of faith). I first wrote about the difference between unconditional love and unconditional positive regard in my first book, Cobwebs and Ugly Wallpaper. The problem is that many of us did not get unconditional love in childhood, we got conditional love instead. Therefore, we now seek unconditional love as adults, especially from our spouses, which leads to chronic disappointment and anger. What were the 'conditions' of love of childhood? Well, whatever was contained in the parents' or other caregivers' Comments (see LVAC above). Children observe the adults around them very carefully and thoroughly. They quickly learn what they are allowed or not allowed to say, do, think, and even feel, based upon the parents' Comments, which were expressed in either their words or their behaviors. These Comments are the conditions of their love for us. Unconditional positive regard on the other hand, unlike unconditional love, simply means benefit of the doubt. While most of us can no longer get unconditional love as adults (again, unless you are a person of faith and get it from God), we can and should be shooting for unconditional positive regard, especially with our spouses and other peers. Save the unconditional love for your children. They need it and should be getting it from us, their parents.

L=Living with pain and failure
The second "L" in the REALADULTS mnemonic stands for the adult skill of living with pain and failure. You might be asking, What else are we supposed to do with pain and failure if not live with it? The answer is that rather than living WITH it, we can choose instead to live it by acting it out in our lives. So there is a fundamental choice we have here: either learn to live with our pain and failure or act it out. An example of living your pain would be having an affair, whereas talking about wanting to have an affair because of feelings of disconnect, alienation and despair would instead be living with your pain instead of acting it out; we must learn to aim for talking and connecting about it, not acting it out.

T=Thank you and I'm sorry (and Tone)
Very simple. I noticed a long time ago that people , especially in marriage, are very bad about being able to say 'Thank you' and 'I'm sorry' to one another. Part of this, I think, is that we come into adulthood and marriage already preloaded with resentments and other hurts from earlier in life that we subconsciously transfer over to our spouses so that we already have less emotionally generosity with them (i.e. less unconditional positive regard) than we would have even with a

perfect stranger. Needless to say, we must work on reversing this. The harder it is for you to say 'Thank you' or 'I'm sorry', the more you will grow stronger and heal inside by forcing yourself to say these two things, especially to those closest to you.

The 'T' in REALADULTS also stands for Tone. Again, simply put: Sometimes our tone can communicate more, for better or worse, than the actual words we use, so we have to watch our tone.

S=Stopping.
This is one that many of us are not good at whatsoever. Oh, most of us certainly have learned how to go go go! That's because in our ultra-competitive society we are taught from an early age to get up, get out there, and perform! It's really no wonder why then, after so many years of childhood schooling, plus any additional schooling or training, then years spent working, that so many people have such a hard time adjusting emotionally to the idea of being retired. In general, we aren't actually very good at being still and not having to perform, and, with that, we perpetuate a sense of disconnect within ourselves: We are only as good as what we can do or what we have achieved, rather than having a baseline of unconditional self-worth. Practice the adult skill of Stopping by first learning to identify and resist the pressure within you that says you must keep moving. Then the goal becomes to eventually learn to overcome that pressure and to experience what it feels like to be tranquil.

CHAPTER 63

LIVING DELIBERATELY (Y)

Do you live deliberately, or reactively?

Whenever I'm talking with someone, I'm always interested in how much of their day-to-day life seems to be "deliberate" versus being dictated by various immediate emotional reactions; the latter is a style of living which we might term "reactive".

For example, let's say a man is feeling disconnected from his spouse; that they are more like roommates than anything else. Let's also say that he's been feeling lots of stress at work or in other areas of his life. He's also got many other pressures and responsibilities, all of which have been feeling overwhelming to him.

The above is an example of a person who has risk factors for some form of non-deliberate, "reactive" life choices. In other words, he is at risk for what some call acting out behaviors.

He may, for example, decide to have an affair, or to use drugs or alcohol to momentarily escape the pressure and disconnect that he feels from his life. Perhaps he may begin to show up late to work or start to procrastinate. His boundaries with others may slowly loosen up in various destructive or self-sabotaging ways, or he might make one or more purchases to temporarily make himself feel better.

These choices are often more accurately described as reactions to internal or external pressures than they are well thought-out, deliberate choices or adult decisions. We tend to know this because these are the very same choices which eventually prove to be damaging to the person's life, including their relationships, their finances, or their physical and emotional health. The point is that ultimately, it is NOT what the person really wants.

So why do we humans do this?

We live reactively for many reasons, including because we are feeling things like disconnect and loss in our lives, fear, anxiety, anger, emptiness, boredom, and other strong emotions.

So what should we be doing about it?

We need to get away from reactive living and we need to get back to deliberate living.

In other words, we need to get back into our real lives, with our real emotions, and our real relationships, and not try to run around and "act" out destructively.

How?

To start with, for example, you are better off taking a walk or throwing yourself into serving your children or other dependents, or perhaps doing something healthy for yourself such as preparing a healthy meal or tackling a task you've been putting off, than you are taking any of the reactive options listed in the example above.

If you're feeling out of sorts, or have free floating anxiety, why not sit down with a pen and paper and list the things that are truly bothering you or that you are worried about?

Maybe you've been procrastinating something important (or lots of things), or maybe you're worried about your physical health and have not followed through with seeing your doctor about it for a basic checkup.

Whatever it is, you're better off identifying it and listing it out and maybe even discussing it with someone than you are ignoring it completely and letting it serve as fuel for some indirect acting out process from all the guilt, anxiety, fear, etc., that's building up inside you.

Whenever we put something off for a long time it has a tendency to take on a power and an insurmountability far beyond the actual, original issue at hand. This is not healthy, neither emotionally nor physically.

You might be surprised how freeing and healing it is to make decisions in your day-to-day life deliberately, where they are based on what you really want in your life versus reactively, where they are based on your fears, worries, or conflicts.

Here are some examples of how to live deliberately:

1) if you've decided to get up earlier to spend time with your family before work or to eat healthier or to get to work earlier, then make it of utmost importance and priority to follow through with your plan

2) if you've decided to do the above, then you will likely need to go to bed earlier; decide what time to go to bed and do it, and don't give in to "just another minute" of reading, television, work, or computer time

3) if you've decided that it would be good for you to make some dietary and exercise changes, then go ahead and deliberately and slowly make those changes for yourself and your health

4) if you've decided to spend more "quality time" with your spouse or significant other, then arrange to do so rather than continuing the cycle of "hello/goodbye" living with them each day-practice LVAC with them

5) if you've decided to tackle a project at home or for your health, then list out the steps you'll need to follow to accomplish these things; now go ahead and make that appointment with your doctor, or visit the home improvement store, or clear off your desk or kitchen table to get started with those bills or the taxes

As you can see, deliberate living is very different from living reactively. The best part is that by doing so regularly, you'll experience greater energy and self-esteem, you'll position yourself to be more in line with who you really are and what you really want, AND you'll free yourself from many of the internal struggles which bind you and cause you to need to escape from your life in the first place.

You'll have, in a word, joy.

CHAPTER 64

HOW TO IDENTIFY PAIN (Y)

We often have no problem identifying physical pain, but when it comes to emotional pain, unless it's something obvious, we're often unaware of it; unaware of the emotional pain that we carry around in our lives and of the impact that it has on our behavior and the choices that we make, including the way we react to things and the words that come out of our mouths.

Some time ago, I observed someone "losing it" with their child at a local Toys-R-Us store. Of course, we all do this from time to time, but it's important to know when we are crossing the line between appropriate behavior, such as helping to correct a child's behavior, and acting out our own pain on that child by overreacting with rage or by directly attacking and undermining the child's self-esteem, perhaps thereby repeating what happened to us when we were children ourselves.

The ways we act out our pain on our children are often the same ways our earliest caregivers acted out THEIR pain on us, which is how we learned it, so we are simply repeating the pattern, never realizing what we are really doing or that it's a cycle that must stop.

We also act out our pain in our relationships with other adults.

How many times have you snapped at your spouse or at other adults in your life, for example a co-worker, sibling, neighbor, or friend, only to later feel guilty or ashamed about it? That was your pain talking.

We humans carry around an awful lot of subconscious pain around with us every day of our lives and we often act it out with our behaviors and our choices without even realizing it.

Here are some examples of behaviors which come from our pain:

-drug and alcohol abuse

-shopping or gambling addiction

-chronic anger or erratic behavior

-procrastinating or avoiding

-self-sabotaging

-ignoring, suppressing, or repressing our feelings

-constantly searching for The Next Big Thing or The Key To Life

-related to above: need for constant stimulation, thrill seeking, or novelty seeking

-regularly engaging in risky behaviors

-lack of true intimacy with others

-inability to hold down a regular job

-narcissism, entitlement, or feeling above everyone else

-needing to habitually control things

-sexual addictions

-lack of follow-through or self-worth

-idealizing and devaluing people (i.e. building them up only to later tear them down)

Here are some examples of where we get our pain from:

-alcoholic or drug addicted parent or parents

-depressed or overly-anxious parent(s)

-absent or neglectful parent(s)

-emotional, physical, or sexual abuse

-emotional role reversal with parents (i.e. parentification of the child)

-related to above: growing up too fast or experiencing too much too soon

-witnessing violence

-poor nutrition and severe lack of other resources and necessities

-chaotic, hectic, inconsistent childhood environment

Every one of us can identify with at least one item from each of these two lists, and for most of us, more than just one. We all carry pain every day, and we expose our lives and the people in our lives to this pain on a regular basis.

The first thing we need to do is to acknowledge that there is a whole other emotional universe under the surface of our lives, one in which there are many leftover feelings and triggers from as far back as childhood, starting with the disappointments and betrayals we experienced with our primary caregivers, up to and including present day hurts and traumatic experiences.

Sometimes we need to have a special person in our lives, or even a few of them, with whom we can regularly talk about our fears, our frustrations, our anxieties, our sadness, our despair, our losses, our insecurities, our shame, our guilt, and all the other feelings which most of us carry around with us without ever really fully knowing about or acknowledging. Some people prefer to journal or use art or other venues to express their pain.

Try to make it a regular practice to somehow process your pain. Put it into words if you can. Your subconscious tries its best to process your pain for you in your dreams at night, but, for most of us, we also need a regular venue in which to identify and to express our pain so that we can be free to live our lives, not our pain.

It's like this: We can either live out our pain and have it unconsciously color everything in our lives, or we can begin to free ourselves by learning how to identify and process the pain so that it doesn't control us.

CHAPTER 65

THE PROBLEM WITH OUR ADDICTIONS (Y)

The reason I put the word addictions in quotes is because I want to talk about a broader issue than what most of us think about when we hear the word addiction; that is, I want to talk about all of us and our addictive behaviors, whatever they might be.

And they might be one or more of the following: shopping, sex, drugs and alcohol, gambling, risky or high adrenaline activities, thrill seeking to feel alive, workaholism, rage, novelty seeking, and self-injurious behaviors (e.g. cutting, burning, scratching), among others. Most of us can identify with at least one item from this list, if not several, or perhaps with other forms of addictive behavior not listed.

The above are things which can make us feel temporarily satiated when we feel empty, or connected and calm when we feel abandoned or lost. For a moment, they address our sense of betrayal or outrage, and they soothe the angst we sometimes feel about the ultimate meaning (or meaninglessness) of our lives.

But the problem with our addictive behaviors is that they ultimately cause further disconnect from ourselves and from our real lives; and that includes the people in our lives such as our children, our spouses, and our friends and neighbors, among others.

The other problem with our addictive behaviors is that they burn up our vital life energy, which is a term I use to describe the combination of two of our most limited natural resources: our time and our energy. If we are spending our time and energy "over there" and "doing that" (i.e. in our acting out, addictive behaviors), then, by definition, we cannot also be "over here" and "doing this" (i.e. in our real lives with the real people in our lives.)

In fact, it's not unusual for somebody to tell me that, soon after they stopped spending their time and energy doing whatever addictive behaviors they were doing, sometimes for years at a time, they realized that they were absolutely exhausted. They also realized just how much energy they were burning, and they could feel the difference in both their energy levels and the time they now had available for other endeavors; ones that they actually wanted in their lives.

We humans regularly try to escape the realities of our lives as well as the pain of our lives via addictive behaviors. It can be extremely difficult to 'live life on life's terms', as has been said before. Who can blame us for trying to escape the pain of life by using these behaviors, especially the ones that are perfectly legal and socially acceptable, such as workaholism or novelty seeking?

Of course, some behaviors are more obviously problematic and destructive, such as drugs and alcohol, infidelity, gambling, or impulsive spending. For the most part, however, many of the people around us, including those who seem to be living absolutely normal, product lives, do, in some form or another, act out addictively, which can be difficult for them to admit.

Yes, you are a good and valuable human being. Yes, you are worthy and honorable. And, yes, you very likely have some addictive behaviors that you use when you are feeling miserable, upset, anxious, angry, worried, overwhelmed, jealous, etc. We must understand that concept of addiction is not just for the clinically obvious, substance-based, DSM-V diagnosable illnesses. The idea is that any time we are experiencing emotional pain, especially when we are consciously unaware of it, we are at risk and vulnerable to acting out that pain with our addictive, destructive behaviors.

Therefore we must come to consciously know, identify, and become conversant with our pain, such that it no longer controls our lives, especially when we are functioning in less than optimal conditions; i.e. when we are feeling tired, hungry, lonely, angry, ashamed, jealous, overwhelmed, anxious, etc. We must learn to acknowledge and to feel our pain, not dwell in it or act it out; the former will give us a chance to live our lives but the latter only our pain.

The bottom line is this: We all have a limited amount of time and energy allotted to us, and if we spend these resources pursuing our addictive behaviors, we are not spending them on our real lives. The result will be eventual disconnect from both ourselves and from our loved ones and the risk of troubles in both our work and with other real-life priorities.

Made in the USA
San Bernardino, CA
11 November 2019